"In four short pages a day, take a journey toward the freedom only humility can bring: freedom from pride, from insecurity, and from the torment of comparative thinking. Take the challenge—you won't regret it. *The Humility Project for Men* makes the route clear. Day by day, Ed Welch takes you down the path that will make you more like Christ."

Brad Hambrick, Pastor of Counseling, The Summit Church; author of *Transformative Friendships*

"Sometimes you need someone to reframe something for you—to give you a new way of seeing it. This is what Ed Welch does in *The Humility Project for Men*, and it's a gift. This little book takes a concept that you thought you understood and makes it three-dimensional."

Marc Davis, Associate Area Director for Renewal, Serge

"On this daily walk, Ed Welch offers wise love at its finest. The nastiness of pride is unmasked, and the manliness of humility is unveiled. Best of all, Jesus gets the praise for remaking us to be settled and strong under him. I can't wait to invite the men I shepherd to join me on this path. Thank you, Ed, for living and mapping the way."

Greg Norfleet, Director of Counseling Ministry, Briarwood Presbyterian Church

"Rather than reading mere words on a page, imagine Ed is in the room with you as a gentle, tender father leading and helping you draw near to the humility of Christ. While pride is always lurking and luring us, it is the humility of Christ that truly captures the heart. Humility is the way of the Christian because it is the way of Christ."

Nathan Sawyer, Pastor, Grace Church Memphis; online instructor, CCEF

"This is a gem of a book, filled with wisdom. Ed traces the silent thread of humility (or its lack) through our sins and our virtues. It might be written for men, but it's for everyone!"

Paul E. Miller, Author of *A Praying Church* and *J-Curve: Dying and Rising With Christ in Everyday Life*

"In a world where humility often feels scarce, Ed Welch offers men a rich, grace-filled invitation to rediscover this vital virtue. Drawing from years of counseling experience and deep biblical insight, he helps readers see humility not as weakness but as Christlikeness—continually lifting our eyes to Jesus, the true model of a humble heart."

Jonathan D. Holmes, Interim Executive Director, CCEF

"These devotional reflections on humility are vintage Ed Welch. In this book, familiar Scriptures speak with fresh urgency and clarity and the many vivid stories bring theology to life. Things we thought we knew about pride and humility are revisited in ways that draw us into personal engagement with Christ. This is a humility project that will bless everyone's soul."

Steve Midgley, Executive Director, Biblical Counselling UK

"Ed Welch shepherds us gently toward our humble Savior. Through vivid portraits of God's humility, the Spirit stirred my heart and challenged my pride, freeing me to love more deeply. This devotional is a timely gift to the church—inviting us to slow down, listen, and live more like the One who is gentle and lowly in heart."

Robert K. Cheong, Executive Director, Gospel Care Ministries; author of *Restore: Changing How We Live and Love* and *Restoration Story: Why Jesus Matters in a Broken World*

THE HUMILITY PROJECT FOR MEN

THE HUMILITY PROJECT FOR MEN

THE WAY TO STRENGTH, HONOR, AND CONTENTMENT

Edward T. Welch

New Growth Press, Greensboro, NC 27401
newgrowthpress.com

Cover Design: Tim Green, Tiny Giant Co
Interior Typesetting and Ebook: Lisa Parnell, lparnellbookservices.com

ISBN: 978-1-64507-593-6 (paperback)
ISBN: 978-1-64507-594-3 (ebook)

Library of Congress Cataloging-in-Publication Data

Names: Welch, Edward T., 1953– author
Title: The humility project for men : the way to honor, strength, and contentment / Edward T. Welch.
Description: Greensboro, NC : New Growth Press, [2026]
Identifiers: LCCN 2025041957 (print) | LCCN 2025041958 (ebook) | ISBN 9781645075936 paperback | ISBN 9781645075943 ebook
Subjects: LCSH: Humility—Religious aspects—Christianity | Christian men—Religious life
Classification: LCC BV4647.H8 W45 2026 (print) | LCC BV4647.H8 (ebook)
LC record available at https://lccn.loc.gov/2025041957
LC ebook record available at https://lccn.loc.gov/2025041958

Printed in Colombia

30 29 28 27 26   1 2 3 4 5

CONTENTS

❧ ❧ ❧

If you ask me what is the essential thing
in the religion and discipline of Jesus Christ,
I shall reply: first humility, second humility, and third humility.
—Saint Augustine

If anyone would like to acquire humility,
I can, I think, tell him the first step.
The first step is to realize that one is proud.
And a biggish step, too.
—C. S. Lewis, "Pride" in Mere Christianity

When Christ calls a man, he bids him come and die.
—Dietrich Bonhoeffer

For the LORD takes pleasure in his people;
he adorns the humble with salvation.
—Psalm 149:4

❧ ❧ ❧

WELCOME

Humility is probably not your first choice of essential topics. A few weeks of practice in being lowly does not make anyone's to-do list. But Scripture and the wise men who have gone before us tell a different story. They make their plea—our honor, strength, contentment, and rest depend on humility, as do all of our relationships. It is the door into all virtues, and its opposite—pride—brings us into all vices. The ancient sages urge you to enter in.

Augustine wrote, "If you ask me what is the essential thing in the religion and discipline of Jesus Christ, I shall reply: first humility, second humility, and third humility."[1] His autobiography, *Confessions*, is not a story of achievements. It is a story of a man whose pride authorized him to follow his own passions above all else, the destruction it caused, and the sanity that came from humility before God and faith in Christ.

Jonathan Edwards wrote, "The first and worst cause of errors that abound in our day and age is spiritual pride."[2] Charles Spurgeon wrote of his "darling sin" of pride."[3] C. S. Lewis wrote of pride often, and he dedicated a chapter to pride in *Mere Christianity*.

The church's humility project has had many contributors over the years. Here is a small sample:

Thomas à Kempis, *The Imitation of Christ*
Richard J. Foster, *Learning Humility*
Grant Macaskill, *The New Testament and Intellectual Humility*
Kent Dunnington, *Humility, Pride, and Christian Virtue Theory*
Dennis R. Edwards, *Humility Illumined*

Jerry Bridges, *The Blessing of Humility*
J. Lanier Burns, *Pride and Humility at War*
Gavin Ortlund, *Humility: The Joy of Self-Forgetfulness*

This short book is another contribution. In it, I will try to respect your time by getting right to the point. Yet since mere knowledge is not enough, after each daily reading I have inserted prompts that will slow you down: *circle, reflect, pray, talk*. I found these steps helpful as I studied humility, so I am passing them on. I found the reminders to talk to the Lord and to talk to other people to be especially helpful.

What surprised me as I was preparing to write this devotional is that humility is an activist. It energizes. It does not simply sit around and defer to others. For example, I am a responder by nature. I ask my wife, "What would *you* like to do?" Part of that style is most likely connected to me not wanting to take responsibility for a less-than-good time if we enacted my suggestion. A few months into this project I suggested, "Let's . . ." If she was struggling and I contributed to some of her disappointment, I would ask her to talk about it, own what was mine, and pray with her. While that all seems ordinary, it is also raw spiritual power. Left to myself, I am inclined toward self-pity when my wife is not thoroughly pleased with me. I have been surprised by the strength of humility, and I love it.

Meditating on spiritual realities feels like a luxury for which we don't have time. But there are some matters of such importance that we can't let the opportunity pass. Welcome to a well-worn tradition that includes kings, prophets, sages, and—as is God's style—ordinary people like us.

ೞ ೞ ೞ

DAY 1
THIS IS HUMILITY

Humble yourselves before the Lord,
and he will exalt you.
—James 4:10

Being a man is complicated. Being *any* kind of human being is complicated, but today men are feeling the complexities—younger men even more. Relationships are harder. Our best efforts don't seem to be enough. Successful long-term relationships are rare. Steady work has been replaced by uncertainty. In order to feel alive, we are left with online jolts from gaming, intrigue, indignation, and sensuality, each adding their own touch of chaos. Meanwhile, many men feel increasingly nonessential; "useless" and "worthless" are closing in.

Is this really the right time to think about humility?[4]

I recently talked with a man who radically owned what he brought to a bad marriage that was headed for divorce. The only thing he and his wife shared was the skill of blaming the other. Then he saw his pride, perhaps for the first time, and he confessed that he had been living for himself—not God, and not his wife. He was only stating the obvious, but pride is too weak to say such things. His wife was stunned and softened. A path to reconciliation opened. Humility is apparently quite powerful.

You might think that humility makes you even smaller. Your impression of what it means to be humble is that you have to take whatever nastiness and injustice come your way. An old saint put it this way: "You and the donkey must be alike. The donkey says nothing when he is beaten."[5] Be a human punching bag, or better, be *nothing* so people don't even notice when they walk over you. Never judge, because you are much worse than that person. Overall, talk less, give up your place in line, say, "Yes, whatever you say, you are right," and do what the other person prefers rather than give your own preferences. Humility means you point to heaven whenever somebody says something nice about you. If you are suspicious when you consider humility, you have good reason to be, even though none of these reasons is accurate.

Humility could be easily dismissed until you know these two things:

1. The alternative is ugly. If not humility, then pride, and pride is a killer. It clings to most everything that has brought misery to your relationships. It empowers insecurity, unchecked anger, resentment, despair, hopelessness, and, much worse, distance from God.
2. Humility might seem weak until you know that God became man. Once you learn that your Creator—who is quite impressive and no wallflower—is the humble Servant, humility can catch your attention. It turns out to be the *only* way to become a person of influence, settled in your own skin, deeply and truly human.

WHAT IS HUMILITY?

Humility is first before God, rather than before people. *Humility means that you live before God, dependent on him, with a heart that listens.* Our minds tend to think first of the distasteful possibilities of humility toward other people and the potential injustices we might have to ignore. Don't go there.

Start with God. Humility is to rest in God alone, listen to what he says, learn from him, and respond to him. From that place, humility takes action, and other people notice. Here are a few places where you will find it in Scripture.

"I am not worthy" (Luke 7:6). Jesus "marveled" at the faith of a Gentile centurion who spoke these words (Luke 7:9). This man understood Jesus's greatness, his own need, and the extravagant gift that he requested, which was that Jesus would give someone life. He was among the first in the New Testament to understand the grace of God. Say these words every day and your community will marvel too. In what is ahead, this will also appear as a rhetorical question: Who am I (that you, Jesus, would know and care about me, which you most certainly do)?

"My Lord and my God" (John 20:28). Humility is to know that Jesus is over all creation. He alone is worthy of your loyalty and obedience. You can call him "my Lord" and "my God."

"Speak, for your servant hears" (1 Samuel 3:10). Humility is to hear God's voice above all others, to seek out that voice, and to do what he says. This means we have to be lower and *under* God.

"Help." This appears throughout Scripture, and men are notoriously bad at saying it. The Northern Kingdom of Israel fell, in part, because men didn't ask God for help (Hosea 7:14).

"Thank you." Humility is to know that what you have accomplished or any good you have received is not a result of your own greatness but is a gift from God that you did nothing to deserve. "Every good and perfect gift is from above" (James 1:17 NIV).

> "My soul finds rest in God alone" (Psalm 62:1 NIV 1984). Humility renounces the human project of reputation and status, which never finds a place of rest. You don't have to always prove yourself. You don't have to be somebody who hides your failures, because you are secure in the accomplishments of Jesus on your behalf.
>
> "He [Jesus] must increase, but I must decrease" (John 3:30). These are the words of John the Baptist, of whom Jesus said there was none greater. John was bold, unmoved by rejection, and he stood with courage against injustices. Though he was willing to be anonymous, even today most everyone knows his name.
>
> "Jesus, I need you." The psalmist says it well: "As for me, I am poor and needy, but the Lord takes thought for me" (Psalm 40:17). Other than, "I need sex," "I need a drink," or "I need a break," men rarely speak about needing anyone or anything. *Dependence* is awkward enough. *Need* is offensive. But when we grow into maturity, this is what wise men say. When you prize the words *poor* and *needy*, good things happen. It is the way you are created.

Humility, we fear, is the way of doormats and losers, but we are misguided. Humility replaces inadequacy and insecure bravado with confidence. Humility is the path of the resilient, bold, sturdy, strong, even-tempered, confident, and those at rest. It is the way of wise, daily decisions and peace in relationships. It is the way of freedom. The secret within humility is that our lives no longer teeter on our fragile egos but rest on something much firmer—Christ himself. Humility is to know that God has revealed himself most fully in Jesus Christ, who is in charge and lives to serve you even at this moment. He is the humble Servant God.

ᔓᔕ ᔓᔕ ᔓᔕ

CIRCLE (write, underline, or highlight): One way to engage with humility is to physically circle at least one thing that is important to you from this devotional. What stands out? This reading is longer than the others, and there is a lot here, so you might want to circle everything that stands out to you. Be sure to circle *humility means that you live before God.*

REFLECT: Do you have other hesitations? Write down some reasons that this project is worthy and important. If you want to see how this moves toward something uninhibited and bold, you can temporarily skip ahead and read Day 41, "You First."

PRAY: What do you want to ask of the Lord?

TALK: Talk to one person about what you are reading.

If you are reading this book with a group, ask one person to pray for you as you go through the coming weeks.

DAY 2
THIS IS PRIDE

Those who walk in pride he is able to humble.
—Daniel 4:37

Everyone who is arrogant in heart is an abomination to the Lord.
—Proverbs 16:5

Pride stands against humility, and it is formidable.

"I am really proud of my lawn (my work, how I fixed the faucet, . . .)." This is satisfaction in a job well done, and it is *not* what God identifies as pride. If there is such a thing as *good* pride, this is it. When you play a game, you try to win. You are supposed to do that, and the game would be less fun for everyone if you didn't.

Pride has larger aspirations. Pride wants to "make a name" for itself (Genesis 11:4). Just a little better, a little bit above. Puffed up. It always compares, always judges. Finding fault makes you feel bigger. You might find it strange how other people seem to wrong you quite a bit, but you never seem to wrong them. All this is about image more than character. What do other people see? What are their opinions of you? A winner or a loser? Notice how body image is a concern for men as much as it is for women.

Don't expect to find it in saying, "I am the greatest!" Anyone who says that is either joking or feels like the worst. Find it when you feel small, insecure, near the precipice of depression because you thought you would be somebody by now. Find it in your heart, where you store those things that are most important to you, in daydreams of accolades, in a need to be irresistible to someone else, in resentments against those who treat you as someone less than you believe you are.

No matter how we feel, if pricked with a pin, out we come—me, my desires, my wants, what I deserve. Where pride is present, the interests of others are second, and we often don't get to the second thing on our list. No wonder our relationships can be on life support. And our relationship with the Lord is as well. No wonder we can go for significant stretches without really needing God. Once you know what you are looking for, you can find pride everywhere, in everyone—even in yourself.

Watch Jesus's disciples. As they follow him to Jerusalem, where he will be crucified, they are concerned about other matters: "A dispute also arose among them, as to which of them was to be regarded as the greatest" (Luke 22:24). It's amazing that Jesus did not absolutely freak out on them. Pride caused the Devil to be the Devil,[6] and God hates it (Proverbs 8:13). But Jesus patiently used this as an occasion to teach the disciples how to grow into true greatness.

WHERE YOU CAN FIND PRIDE HIDING

Arrogance and pride are natural to us. Consider three places where they hide.

Anger. Pride's most common face is anger. It says, "I am right." The other person is the problem. Watch for anger's massive range: violence, rage, threats, blame, judging, jealousy, silence, cursing, slander, sarcasm, and complaining, even if these exist only in your own mind. They all share this: you are the judge, jury and executioner. God is not in it.

Sensuality. Pride also shows up in all sexual imagination and acts that are outside the boundaries God has established. Pride says, "Nothing is more important than my desires." You desire physical pleasure, and you desire to be desired—God is not allowed in. Perhaps you felt guilty at first, but you can easily erode guilt if you practice enough. After all, some things God asks of you are unreasonable, such as setting boundaries on your desires and loving people who aren't loving you very well.

Anxiety and shame. Pride is harder to see within these experiences because you already feel small and low. Neither anxiety nor shame is prideful in itself. They can both be sheer misery. But pride is apparent when your anxiety and shame can't hear God's words. Although those feelings seem to be so loud that no one's love could break in, God is not just anyone. Even rocks and trees can hear his voice.

Pride has different faces. There is arrogant judgment, unleashed desires, and even isolation and withdrawal. This diverse group gathers when your heart has sealed off a piece of itself, and God is not in it.

Yet even now you can engage the fight. Say, "speak Lord, your servant is listening." Try actually saying it out loud.

ꟹ ꟹ ꟹ

CIRCLE: What stands out to you?

REFLECT: Think about the times you are angry, afraid, or despondent. Describe how your own pride might be at work during those times.

PRAY: What do you want to say to the Lord? What do you want to ask?

TALK: Talk to someone about what you are thinking. If someone is praying for you, update them.

DAY 3

PRIDE IS . . . BIZARRE

The king [Nebuchadnezzar] answered and said, "Is not this great Babylon, which I have built by my mighty power as a royal residence and for the glory of my majesty?"
—*Daniel 4:30*

A child hits his younger brother. His wrongdoing is obvious, and his mother tells him that he must ask forgiveness. What could be more natural than asking forgiveness? But the words simply cannot come from his mouth. His pride will accept *any* discipline other than saying "Will you forgive me?" This, of course, is beyond belief. Four words—just say it. They are suitable and right. But pride hates going lower. Pride has an irrational loathing of humility and even of reason itself.

A teenager wants independence because they know what is best. Of course, that teenager is also quite dependent on his or her family for survival. The bemused parent cannot even think of words that would bring sense to the teen.

A husband and wife quarrel over which of them is right, and each wants the last word. Gradually, they regress to schoolyard talk: "You are just like your mother!" "Oh yeah? You're sooo dumb." The less-than-human snarling and growling come next.

Yes, we can look like something less than human in our pride. Perhaps you know the story of Nebuchadnezzar, the king of Assyria during Daniel's time. After he irrationally took credit for Babylon's glory, we witness how pride is more suited to an animal than a human. For seven years, this king roamed the fields like an ox, with grass for his food. God let the king's inner ox reveal itself. Only when he humbled himself before the Lord did he look like a man again (Daniel 4:29–37).

Pride is one of the foremost ways of describing sin. It is against God and other people. It is also supremely bizarre and incongruous for humans, who by nature are dependent and have accomplished nothing in themselves to justify their own enthronement. Pride is irrational. God's design is that we live under him. God rules—not us (Daniel 4:26). We live only by the "immeasurable riches of his grace" (Ephesians 2:7), and yet pride has set up camp in every human heart. Though created by God and fully dependent on him for everything, we live as though we have earned our way to the top.

Pride is a summary of all sin. It is also truly odd. It is unnatural, stupid, and less than human. Our goal is not simply to be concerned about outbreaks of pride; it is to find pride absurd, a ridiculous feature of our human existence that will someday be no more. Pride, when seen clearly, is the humiliation of our souls.

We are created with royalty in our veins, but *Christ* is King, and everything we have with any eternal value is his gift to us. As royalty, we take on the ways of the King: "Let each of you look not only to his own interests, but also to the interests of others" (Philippians 2:4). So we set out for humility, which turns out to be wonderfully human and surprisingly powerful.

ꟸ ꟸ ꟸ

CIRCLE: What is important for you here?

REFLECT: Have you noticed how "disrespect" is a near-lethal injury to many men? Also notice how those who are strong—like superheroes, gunslingers, and black belts—don't have to boast or display their strength. Humility rests in the unbeatable strength of God and the army that accompanies him, which makes you less reactive to criticism. Can you imagine what that might look like in your own life?

PRAY: Talk to the Lord about your foolish pride.

TALK: Talk to someone about what you are thinking. Would this be a good time to ask for prayer because you need Jesus to keep you from being an animal?

HUMILITY BEFORE GOD

When Scripture speaks about humility,
it does not begin with how to walk humbly before other people.
Humility in life depends first on humility before God.

ꕥ ꕥ ꕥ

DAY 4
HUMILITY, FAITH, AND FEAR

The fear of the LORD is instruction in wisdom,
and humility comes before honor.
—Proverbs 15:33

Let's say you want to start a self-improvement project, so you begin working on the fruits of the Spirit: "love, joy, peace, patience, kindness, goodness, faithfulness, gentleness, self-control" (Galatians 5:22–23). Twenty years later, you have made it halfway through the list, and humility isn't even on it. Humility, however, is not just one of many good gifts. Humility is necessary for life. Only in humility will you be able to have enduring relationships and care well for those you love. More than that, *only in humility can you enter God's house*.

The Lord says, "I dwell in the high and holy place, and also with him who is of a contrite and lowly spirit" (Isaiah 57:15). The lowly know that their own resources are not enough, and they need what Jesus gives. In other words, if you don't need Jesus, you don't have Jesus. Humility is at the heart of *faith* and *trust*, and these are at the center of our response to Christ. "By grace you have been saved through faith" (Ephesians 2:8). In contrast, trusting in yourself and your own righteousness is at the heart of pride (Luke 18:9).

Keep in mind these key words that cluster around humility: *faith*, *trust*, and *dependence*. Each means you need what Jesus has and *only* he has. You were created to depend on him and listen to his Word. The work ahead is much more than a self-improvement exercise. Humility reminds us that life with Christ is rooted in what someone else has done on our behalf. God, in Jesus Christ, came and died to find you and bring you to himself.

Now consider one more word—*fear*, or *fear of the Lord*. The passage from Proverbs 15 matches this phrase with humility. It sounds ominous, but it is the entrance into all wisdom. The basic idea is that you fear what controls you. It will be the loudest voice in the room. If you are controlled by God, you will hear his voice in Scripture and learn how to do relationships, work, and rest the way God intended them to be done. If you are controlled by anything else—personal reputation, being loved, money, entertainment, pleasure—then you will be restless and dissatisfied. Those are chaotic voices that always want more.

The fear of the Lord reminds us that we live under God rather than have a side job of building our own little kingdoms and listening when it is convenient. His voice stands out from the others, and we listen. The fear of the Lord also adds a dash of trembling and awe. When humans catch a glimpse of God's greatness, they are undone. When Jesus's disciples glimpsed God's glory shining from Jesus, "they fell on their faces and were terrified" (Matthew 17:6). In fact, this is how the whole world will respond when Jesus appears again. But for we who have put our trust in him, Jesus comes, touches us, and says, "Rise, and have no fear" (17:7). In future chapters this will reappear as we consider the word *holy*.

All these words join together when you know that God is great and you need him. They all say, "Lord, I'm listening." This is the way you first *come* to him, and this is how you *walk* with him. It is the only path to honor. *Humility is voluntary submission to God alone.*

Now talk to the Lord about this. If humility is first about how you live before God, you need to talk to him rather than merely learn new information.

Consider the words of King David:

> May all who seek you rejoice and be glad in you; may those who love your salvation say continually, "Great is the Lord!" (Psalm 40:16)

Speak the words "Great is the Lord" out loud. That captures it. It is called *worship*, which is another of humility's companions. It will be your sanest and most settled moment of the day, and the fruit of the Spirit will be on its heels.

ᔓᔕ ᔓᔕ ᔓᔕ

CIRCLE: When you understand something well, you have more than one word for it. Humility travels with faith, trust, dependence, fear of the Lord, wisdom, and honor. Each word adds more color. All of them rest in what Jesus has done for us. What strikes you as important from this devotion?

REFLECT: Take time to try to summarize what you read. The main point is that humility shares space with a number of words, and it is at the center of Scripture.

PRAY: What do you want to say to the Lord? What do you want to ask? This would be a good time to ask God to teach you what growing in "the fear of the Lord" would look like every day.

TALK: Talk to one person about what you are learning. This will help you to put this devotion into your own words, and it will help the other person as you speak about matters of the heart.

DAY 5
GOD IS GREAT

Then the LORD answered Job out of the whirlwind and said: "Who is this that darkens counsel by words without knowledge? Dress for action like a man; I will question you, and you make it known to me."
—Job 38:1–3

Humility is your response to the greatness of God. A sixty-two-year-old man demonstrated this at a men's group. His daughter had died after a five-year battle with cancer. He and his wife had lost their daughter, their three young grandchildren had lost their mother, and their son-in-law had lost his wife. Two months had passed since the funeral, and he was asked to say a few words in the group. After five minutes or so, in which he spoke of his grief and God's strength, he ended with the words of Job: "The LORD gave, and the LORD has taken away; blessed be the name of the LORD" (Job 1:21). This was a high point of humility, and, of course, we all wanted to be just like this man. We also wanted to know the secrets of the man who first spoke these words. Job is our Old Testament model of wisdom.

Job wanted God to explain why a good man was experiencing so much suffering. In response, the Lord actually spoke to him, and when you hear the very words of God, from his mouth, person to person, it is impossible *not* to listen. What you hear will usually surprise you, and in his conversation with Job, the Lord was true to form. It turned out that God asked *Job* the questions, and through them Job learned that God was, indeed, the great God over all.

Consider a few of those questions. Remember that Hebrew fathers have a history of asking questions of their children around the dinner table as a way to instruct them. Love is evident; humility—the fear of the Lord—is the goal.

> Where were you when I laid the foundation of the earth? Tell me, if you have understanding. Who determined its measurements—surely you know! Or who stretched the line upon it? On what were its bases sunk, or who laid its cornerstone, when the morning stars sang together and all the sons of God shouted for joy? (Job 38:4–7)

After 120 or so verses of this, Job learned humility. He responded,

> I'm convinced: You can do anything and everything. Nothing and no one can upset your plans. . . . You told me, "Listen, and let me do the talking. Let me ask the questions. *You* give the answers." I admit I once lived by rumors of you; now I have it all firsthand—from my own eyes and ears! I'm sorry—forgive me. I'll never do that again, I promise! (Job 42:2, 4–6 MSG)

You are designed to live in a world in which God is God and you are not. That sounds simple, but it is a lifelong project to live it out. For Job, it began when he learned that God doesn't miss a thing—not one injustice, not one tear.

Come close and hear God's words to Job. As you are brought into the cadence of God's questions, you notice that he speaks to you, even as you remember that he asks these questions of his favorite people. You find yourself responding, "You, indeed, are great." Call it humility, or worship, or prayer.

ꕥ ꕥ ꕥ

CIRCLE: What is most important for you to remember from this devotion?

REFLECT: Read a section of God's questions (Job 38–41). They are God's words to you. What is your response?

PRAY: Speak your response to the Lord. What do you want to ask him?

TALK: Talk to someone about this.

DAY 6
IF THE LORD WILLS

Come now, you who say, "Today or tomorrow we will go into such and such a town and spend a year there and trade and make a profit"— yet you do not know what tomorrow will bring. What is your life? For you are a mist that appears for a little time and then vanishes. Instead you ought to say, "If the Lord wills, we will live and do this or that."

—James 4:13–15

Today, James has some instruction for you about how to live your best life.

We go into every day with certain expectations. We want to be somewhere on time, get things done, work on a project that we enjoy, relax and not be bothered. The greater the expectations, the greater the collateral damage. The more important our plans are to us, the more we will be ticked off by a child, spouse, roommate, neighbor, slow driver, or coworker who interferes with them. The greater the expectations, the greater the profanity, and the greater the chance that we will love our own agenda more than love other people.

You choose how you live. Will it be "if the Lord wills," or "my will"? Humility says, "If the Lord wills," or, "I am yours." But independence runs strong in us. Too often our natural way of thinking about God is that he is busy, and we are busy. So we both go about our day, meet up for a quick "hello," and then do it again the next day. The truth, of course, is that God is very close and very much in and over all things.

This passage from James is especially about money and work—the sector of our lives we believe is uniquely our own. It sounds so familiar. "Today I will do this, tomorrow I will do that." Perhaps you add, "Lord, bless me," meaning, "Let me make more money."

Imagine how your life would be different if you began your day by praying, "Here is what I hope to do today, but you are God. I want to rest in you and your will when I face the inevitable disappointments, frustrations, and inconveniences. I believe your ways are good." The inconveniences in our days are not interruptions to God's plan; instead, they help us learn to walk humbly with him.

Let's say the day does not go according to your plan. In the past, you would have muttered something under your breath if you were in public or thrown a fit if you were in private. But this time, you come back to your spiritual senses and say, "Your will be done."

Imagine it. To casual observers, you seem less prone to the anger that can leave you so thoughtless and destructive. Meanwhile, God himself, spiritual beings, and the people around you who know God see a powerful man who fights bravely in the midst of spiritual wars.

Here is something important: This passage is not about you being a slave who just submits to every misery. It is about you standing strong on the solid rock of Jesus Christ, who has assured you that he is with you and has got this. It is about being more fully human, not less. You were created to know and depend on the Lord. Independence holds out promises of life, but it cannot deliver. This passage sets you on a path of real strength.

ග ග ග

CIRCLE: What is important in this devotion for you?

REFLECT: Can you imagine a response to the hassles of the day in which you are not mastered by them? You will hear the word *imagine* again. As a general rule, if you can't imagine it, you won't get there.

PRAY: Speak to the Lord the words, "If it is your will, Father." What do you want to ask him?

TALK: Talk to somebody about what you are learning.

DAY 7
HOLY

Holy, holy, holy, is the Lord God Almighty,
who was and is and is to come!
—*Revelation 4:8*

Holiness is not easy to describe, but it is an important concept to understand. So don't give up on this. One way to get closer to it is to find some analogies and illustrations. Think of something that when you see it, you stop—transfixed—as it seizes your attention. An avalanche cascading down a mountain that is coming closer than you thought. A wave so big that when it crashes under its own weight, you cannot hear the person screaming beside you. A baseball stadium you are seeing for the first time with a green expanse that is . . . amazing. A baby—your baby—just born. You try to talk about it, but you can barely find the words. This is a glimpse of the *holy*. Holy means you are in the presence of something greater than yourself. Indifference is impossible. You have to do something or say something. In the presence of the holy, you initially feel like you do not belong there and you are unworthy. Awe captures it. Something changes within you. *Holy* leaves its mark.

Humility says, "Jesus, you are holy." You are amazed by him, and you look forward to being surprised by God's workmanship in other people. Pride, always humility's opposite, is not easily awed. To be moved by something is to acknowledge its greatness. Pride prefers to be above it all. You will notice pride when you read Scripture and are bored because you have heard it all before. Nothing of interest here.

Entertain me. Though Scripture is the very Word of God, and its pages reveal true life, you find more amazement in activities that are skin deep and sometimes deadly to your soul. Sanity emerges when you insist that Scripture convicts and inspires and when it gets you talking with others.

Holy first appears in Scripture when God comes to Moses in a burning bush. God said, "Do not come near; take your sandals off your feet, for the place on which you are standing is *holy* ground" (Exodus 3:5, emphasis added). The ground was holy because God was there. Heaven had come to earth. The King of heaven and earth was present; the ground was consecrated as holy. In the ancient world, you took your shoes off on such ground. In our era, God has come to us and has never left. After Jesus was raised from the dead, he sent the Spirit who dwells with us. This means that you walk through everyday life with your shoes off.

Watch heavenly beings respond to God's holiness. The divine beings who speak, "Holy, holy, holy" about the risen Jesus also fall down before him, which is what people do when they are overwhelmed with emotion. Look at Moses, who was known for his humility in the face of wicked accusations by the Hebrew people. Once you are in the presence of the Holy One, you are not quite as intimidated by the criticisms of others.

There is, of course, much more to be said. Since God is committed to bringing you close, he has made a way for you to come near to him and share in his holiness. For now, pause when you encounter the word *holy*. Be shaken out of your indifference or the anxieties of your day. God is big, different. His love is not like your father's; it is holy love. His justice is not that of a local magistrate; it is holy justice. *Humility is our natural response to the holiness of God.*

Now you must say something. How could you not? "Lord, you are great. *Holy* great." Or, "You are amazing." And give him your reasons. Then, like Moses, allow his greatness to nudge you further into humility. You could express it this way: "Who are you that you would draw me close and make me your own?"

ೞ ೞ ೞ

CIRCLE: What is meaningful to you? Take the time to circle it.

REFLECT: How would you define *holy*? What helps you understand that God is holy? Is there a story from Scripture that helps you? What would it mean to walk through life with your shoes off?

PRAY: There is a lot to say here. "Jesus, you are holy," or, "Lord, you are great." Try speaking those words out loud to the Lord. Ask the Spirit to bring you further into these biblical stories so they are your own. What else do you want to say to him?

TALK: Talk to or text someone about *holy*.

DAY 8
HOLY JUSTICE

When he [Jesus] was reviled, he did not revile in return;
when he suffered, he did not threaten, but continued
entrusting himself to him who judges justly.
—1 Peter 2:23

Life is different when someone who is strong and loving promises to make things right.

I experienced this once when my ten-year-old sister came home from school in tears. Apparently, a boy in class had said something public and hurtful. I remember saying, "I'll take care of it." I was fourteen and perceived as the powerful big brother. I don't remember what I planned to do, but I do remember reassuring her. Then I remember that she stopped crying immediately and went off to do things that ten-year-old girls do.

This story points to knowing God, your Father who cares for you, and knowing the Son, truly God and truly human, who trusts the Father through all kinds of hard circumstances and invites you to do the same. As the apostle Peter watched Jesus, he was impressed by how Jesus responded to insults, disrespect, plots to arrest him, and the injustices surrounding his suffering and death. Sometimes Jesus would expose the treacherous motives of his enemies; other times he would say little or nothing. The one constant was humble trust. He knew that his Father was the Holy Judge who would make everything right.

Humility takes an interest in what is right and wrong. We care about injustices against ourselves and those we love. Humility does not cast injustices off as no big deal or just try to be the bigger person and overlook them. Instead, you have one of two choices: In pride, you assume that God either doesn't care or will not respond with the ferocity that you believe suits the crime. So you take matters into your own hands, and everyone gets hurt. Or, with Jesus, you place your trust in the Holy Judge and remember that no injustice escapes the Father's notice. Not one. God hears, sees, and acts. Jesus followed this path of humility and trust. Wise men follow his lead as we say, "Father, we trust that you will judge with holy wisdom."

From that secure place of humility and trust, you have room to consider how to respond to those injustices. You will need all your spiritual wits about you as you make decisions that span a range from surprising your enemy with grace to contacting legal authorities. The Psalms will help. They are filled with how God's people entrusted justice to him. Sometimes they entrust perpetrators to God in quiet trust (Psalm 3). Other times they hand them to God with a long list of what has been done against them and their preferences for how God might judge those acts (Psalm 10).

For us, however we respond to injustices, we live *under* the Holy Judge. We bring the case to the one who says, "I'll take care of it," and leave it to him. That frees us to deal with the details of what wise faith and love look like in each situation.

When heaven comes to earth, no one will say, "But . . . but that isn't fair." Instead, you will be stunned by the holy judgments of God. There will be nothing left to say. You will simply take your shoes off, be in awe, fall down, and worship. You will want to embrace him and say, "Lord, you are the Holy Judge, and I love you."

CIRCLE: Circle what is meaningful for you.

REFLECT: How do you respond to personal injustices? How would you like to respond?

PRAY: Talk to the Lord about this: "You, Father, are the Holy Judge, and I trust you." Tell him who and what you entrust to him. Confess: "I have been the judge and jury far too many times. Forgive me."

TALK: Talk to or text one person about this.

DAY 9
SECRET SINS

You have set our iniquities before you,
our secret sins in the light of your presence.
—*Psalm 90:8*

Stop for a moment. You have set out on a path that can change your life. Your relationships will deepen, hints of self-loathing and shame will lift, a steady confidence will settle you. But this will be sabotaged if pieces of you still belong to you alone. Where are you indulging in secret sins? Most of us are.

Think about it. If you tuck away part of your life in some dark, hidden corner, it doesn't seem to be hurting anyone—otherwise it wouldn't be secret. You haven't experienced any consequences yet. And you are becoming comfortable with both the sin and the secretness of it. Why stir it all up now? But God says that secret sins need to be uncovered in the light of his presence. Why? It is the same as being married and having a woman or two on the side. Doing that would mean you have broken a covenant and the marriage you claim to have is not a marriage at all. God uses this exact analogy to describe your relationship with him (Hosea 1–2). He took you as his own, but his love was not quite enough for your expansive ego, so you took on other lovers. You are willing to be under God when it is convenient to you. You are a hypocrite, the very thing you identify and dislike in others.

If you are in love with secret sins, you might as well stop here and eat, drink, and be merry because tomorrow will be worse than today and the next day worse yet. But if you realize that God is holy, you might as well face those details sooner rather than later. Take small steps. God is with you, and God wants you all for himself. He doesn't want to share you with activities and people that will set you on a course to death. If you are willing, do something. Small steps. Speak those dark places to the Lord: "Jesus, I don't even know where to start, but here is my heart. I am trying to open the door." He already knows those places, and it is a joy for him when his people turn toward him and speak honestly. (The next reading is about forgiveness, which is so great that it is also *holy*.)

You probably know what comes next. If you can speak to God about sins that are ultimately against him, then it should be a small step to speak openly to another human, who is also a mess. Choose one trustworthy person. Text him. Tell him you need to talk. One step at a time. But act now. The more you think, the more you will rationalize that your secret is best kept a secret.

If you are not actively hiding sins, learn how to be one of those trusted people. One way to do that is to ask another brother to pray for you where sinful temptations run strong. When you are open about your need for Jesus before other people, you will be gentle when others are open with you. Part of life in God's house is preferring that those we love *not* be wrapped in the coils of death when a small step of openness before God is all it takes to be freed.

Humility is knowing that your God sees your heart. Humility says this to the Lord: "Nothing is hidden from you, and nothing is outside the bounds of your holy forgiveness."

ᔓ ᔓ ᔓ

CIRCLE: Circle what is meaningful to you.

REFLECT: Reflect on a good reason to come into the open.

PRAY: If you are hiding sins, now is a fine time to acknowledge that God knows your heart. Speak to the Lord about your sins. Even if you have no hidden sins, confession is a natural part of each day (Matthew 6:12).

TALK: Talk with a brother about the theme of secret sins.

DAY 10

HOLY CONFESSION, HOLY FORGIVENESS

If you, O Lord, should mark iniquities, O Lord, who could stand?
But with you there is forgiveness, that you may be feared.
—Psalm 130:3–4

I have heard forgiveness of sins presented as bad news and good news: The bad news is that you are a sinner, and the good news is that Jesus forgives sin. But this is not completely accurate. The truth is that only the Spirit of God opens your eyes to your own sin and need for God's rescue. So even seeing your own sin is exceptionally good news. Once blinded eyes are open, you have evidence of God's care for you. If you don't see that you are a sinner, it doesn't matter that God forgives and rescues because you have no need of forgiveness or rescue. Of course, that blindness is deadly. *The truly bad news comes when you cannot identify any sin in your own life*. In that condition, you can be certain that humility is not yet in sight.

Psalm 130 is about anguish so severe that the psalmist feels as though he is already in the grip of death. At such a moment, he needs powerful and encouraging words, and he needs them immediately. What were the words of rescue? "With you [God] there is forgiveness." You can be sure of it. The psalmist learned of *holy* forgiveness, which is unlike any human forgiveness you could imagine. The word *feared* gives it away. The psalmist is amazed that God forgives without our groveling or making promises we can't keep. Instead, his forgiveness is like his love. He loves you because he is love. He doesn't love you because you have finally become worthy of his love. And he also forgives you because that is who he is—he delights in forgiving you when you ask. He does not forgive because you have finally remediated yourself and swear to never sin again.

While humans have a limit to how much they forgive, holy forgiveness has no limits and belongs to God alone. Perhaps you remember when the apostle Peter asked Jesus a question: "'Lord, how often will my brother sin against me, and I forgive him? As many as seven times?' Jesus said to him, 'I do not say to you seven times, but seventy-seven times'" (Matthew 18:21–22). In saying this, Jesus gives a little glimpse into the heart of God. When you come to him, he always forgives. And this is where *holy* is so important. We tend to think that God is like a good person—he is nice but he has his limits. He forgives the occasional loss of temper, but he doesn't forgive sins that leave a trail of human destruction. That sounds reasonable, but it is not holy. *Holy* causes you to take your shoes off as you would in the presence of the Holy King. Or you can honor the Lord's forgiveness of you by saying "thank you."

One of the many surprises in Scripture is God bringing you into his holiness and making you holy in him. You will see this when you do something that has his power all over it. Confession of sin is holy. It is the work of the Holy Spirit in you. Confession should be common. "All have sinned"—that is no surprise (Romans 3:23). But it is still stunning. Since sins are first against God, your confession begins with him. That will give you the courage to confess to another person who is a sinner just like you.

All of this is good. To acknowledge sin can be hard, but the results are spectacular. When you are actively confessing your sins before the Lord, you will immediately be less reactive, thin-skinned, and angry when criticized. When you have already confessed sins to the Lord, you have preempted the criticisms of others. You have confessed matters that are much more serious than they imagine, so now you are free to . . . listen.

Humility means that you live before God, dependent on him, with a heart that listens and believes.

ꕤ ꕤ ꕤ

CIRCLE: Circle what is meaningful.

REFLECT: Why is it so hard to acknowledge that we are sinners? What sin is the Holy Spirit convicting you of today?

PRAY: Speak your sins to the Lord and be sure to speak your thanks for forgiveness that is assured in the death and resurrection of Jesus. As Eugene Peterson writes, "The only way to get out of the cramped world of the ego and into the large world of God is through prayer."[7]

TALK: Talk to or text one person.

DAY 11
BAD COMPLAINING

The LORD said to Moses, "How long will these people treat me with contempt?"
—Numbers 14:11 NIV

When he walked in the door, the first thing he did was yell at the dog—the stereotype of a man who feels powerless and wants to exert power over *something*. Better the dog than his spouse, children, friends, or roommates, but all the same, the scene was an ugly one. The dog, of course, was not the problem. It was the people at work, the kids, the bills, the grudges, and everything but the dog. The world had not cooperated in the way he expected it would. You can be sure that he didn't begin the day by praying, "Father, your will be done."

Israel experienced a day when all did not go as planned. They had just sent scouts into the land God promised them, and those men came back with a mixed report. The land was, indeed, rich and fertile. It bore clusters of grapes that required two men to carry them. It was also occupied by people who were big, strong warriors. The majority report was that the occupying people were too powerful to overcome. "And all the people of Israel grumbled against Moses and Aaron" (Numbers 14:2).

Grumbling and complaining are a regular part of a day when something interferes with our plans. We might respond with a profane gesture, making a ruckus online, venting to a coworker, or muttering to no one in particular. We all have our own ways of complaining. This particular complaint is a bad one because God is not in it. Instead of going to God, you are grumbling *against* God.

Remember that humility begins with knowing God, living under him, and listening to what he says. This means you are actually speaking with him and asking for help and grace. At first, you wouldn't think that a little complaining has anything to do with God, which is exactly the point. All of life is lived before God and reveals our hearts toward him. What feels like a little complaining about other people or life in general is in truth complaining against God. He is, after all, the one who is in charge and over all things.

Israel seemed to have good reason for their complaining. They had trekked through the desert only to find that the land promised to them was occupied by professional warriors. But look more closely. Their hearts said, "You, God, have not served us well." This is why the Lord tells Moses and Aaron that the people were not grumbling and complaining against them. The people had rejected God. They wanted to trade him in for Pharaoh. It felt like fear. It sounded like complaining. But it was contempt against the Holy One. Uberpride.

Humility is first before God. The problem is that you often think that everything is fine between you and God. You live your life while he is busy ruling the world. Since we all tend to be blind to how we judge God, this story about Israel is especially good for our soul. It reminds us that the inconveniences and troubles of life expose the truth about our relationship with him. Watch for your frustration and impatience when no one sees. Notice your private thoughts and imaginations. Just because you are not yelling at God does not mean that you are not yelling about God.

A bad complainer thinks his complaining is not personal. After all, he is not saying anything to God, which is the point. He is only yelling at the dog. But look deeper and you will see that he is yelling at God. He stands *over* the God who carried our judgment on himself and died. He should be ashamed.

Complaining, of course, is an ideal occasion for confession of sin. It is very good news to say with David in Psalm 51:4, "against you,

you only, have I sinned." Any opportunity to know holy forgiveness will encourage your heart. Just be sure to keep the conversation with God going until it ends in genuine thankfulness for his forgiveness.

When thankfulness has the last word, you are headed toward humility.

ぐ ぐ ぐ

CIRCLE: Circle what is important.

REFLECT: Bad complaining is easily justified, but look carefully and discover that you stand in judgment over the world and over God. Look for this bad complaining and enjoy confessing it.

PRAY: Talk to the Lord about this. Speak your thanks for God's holy patience.

TALK: Are you talking to someone—anyone?

DAY 12
GOOD COMPLAINING

God, God . . . my God! Why did you dump me miles from nowhere?
Doubled up with pain, I call to God all the day long.
No answer. Nothing. I keep at it all night, tossing and turning.
And you! Are you indifferent, above it all?
—Psalm 22:1–3 MSG

These verses demonstrate how God wants you to speak to him when life is hard. Direct. Honest. Even accusing him of things that are not quite true. He wants *you*, and he is pleased when you come in raw and transparent. He doesn't want a sanitized version of your innermost thoughts; he wants the real thing. The problem is that the real you can be covered in so much junk that you aren't even sure where it can be found. So this might take some work. *Humility means that you listen to God, and you speak to him.*

I was in the middle of a late-night panic attack, and I *thought* I did some spiritual work during it. I went to Scripture and tried to think good thoughts that would leave less room for the panicky ones, but it didn't work. Once the anxiety subsided, I realized that though I engaged with Scripture, I didn't engage with Jesus. I never actually just spoke to him about the torture that I felt.

There are two kinds of complaints: the good ones—the ones you speak to God—and the bad ones—the ones you don't take to God. God accused Israel because of their bad complaints. "They do not cry to me from the heart, but they wail upon their beds" (Hosea 7:14). To put it another way, "they swear a blue streak at the alleged cause of their troubles, but they do not call out to me." Knowing *about* God isn't enough—humility depends on you speaking and listening to him. This is how life in his house works. It's what you do while you walk humbly with him.

Speak about anything, everything—the wicked words that a parent spoke years ago but you still carry, or the public failure that makes you cringe when you think about it, or regrets of foolish choices that hold you. Speak about those secret sins. Anything you hide. Fears about death. Fears that your money will run out before you do. The stuff that makes you angry. These are the best things to talk about.

What if you speak and seem to get nothing in return? Speak about that too. The psalmist records his reaction: "'Just my luck,' I said, 'the High God retires just the moment I need him'" (Psalm 77:10 MSG). What you *cannot do* is think for a moment that your complaints are less significant than others' complaints, that you have no right to say anything, or that you are just too bad to be heard. Anything interfering with your honesty with God is sure to have the Devil's fingerprints all over it.

Keep listening after you speak. As in other conversations, you speak and you listen. You might hear his questions: Do you believe that I love you? Do you believe that I care for you? Do you believe that the words of Jesus are true right now? Give an honest answer, and then listen some more.

You thought it was hard to talk to him about secret sins. That may have been the easy part. Those places where you are weak, more vulnerable, less secure, hurt, damaged by others—those will take some time.

ꕤ ꕤ ꕤ

CIRCLE: What is important?

REFLECT: What keeps you from good complaining—speaking the real stuff—to the Lord?

PRAY: Talk to God. Respond to his questions. Keep the conversation going until Jesus is part of it and you end with, "Thank you," or, "You are, indeed, holy." The more words, the better.

TALK: Talk to someone, anyone.

DAY 13

PHARISEE OR TAX COLLECTOR

> [Jesus] told this parable to some who trusted in themselves that they were righteous, and treated others with contempt: "Two men went up into the temple to pray, one a Pharisee and the other a tax collector. The Pharisee, standing by himself, prayed thus: 'God, I thank you that I am not like other men, extortioners, unjust, adulterers, or even like this tax collector. I fast twice a week; I give tithes of all that I get.' But the tax collector, standing far off, would not even lift up his eyes to heaven, but beat his breast, saying, 'God, be merciful to me, a sinner!' I tell you, this man went down to his house justified, rather than the other. For everyone who exalts himself will be humbled, but the one who humbles himself will be exalted."
>
> —*Luke 18:9–14*

In this story, Jesus identifies two very different ways of life. One is the path of greatness; the other way is the path of humiliation. On one path you humble yourself. On the other path you will be humbled. We listen carefully because we are always on one path or the other. There is no third path.

The Pharisee. You go to church, which is where you find the good people. You give money to the church. You are a member in good standing. You have not committed outright adultery. You are better than the Pharisee in this story because you never recount all your good works with the Lord. You like Jesus. You even read books about humility. You don't always make the best decisions, but you can identify a couple of people who do worse than you. You imagine that God, like a bear on the hunt, stops his quest for judgment when he gets to the worst person. Then he goes home. The Pharisee, of course, is lurking in us all. If we can't see the resemblance, we are most likely him.

The tax collector. The other path sounds suspiciously like the path of humiliation and being a nobody, which you were told we would avoid at the beginning. But remember that seeing sin is a very good thing. It is a gift from God that brings us to him and out of our independent-minded stupor. So study this path of a hated outcast who is now among the world's greats. When you grow up, you hope to be like him.

This path has its miseries, as do all paths. You might even wonder if God is picking on you. The psalmists certainly often felt that way. But dig deep into the heart of the tax collector and you find someone who says, "Who am I that you would know me, love me, forgive me, be patient with me, and deliver me from the wrath to come?" (See 1 Thessalonians 1:10) Deep down you have no delusions that you earned God's love. You only received him, with holy thanks.

I once saw my father cry over his sins. He was never unfaithful to my mother or abusive to his children. I don't even know what sins inspired his grief. He said something about selfishness. He was stunned that, after so many years of following Jesus, he could live for himself. And he wept. Prior to that moment I loved and appreciated my father. He was average according to most any metrics, but I knew he cared, and I had seen his servant's heart. After that moment, I saw a great man and I hoped that one day I would be like him. I have seen many men cry over their own troubles, and I have seen men cry over the sins of those they loved, but my father is the only man I have witnessed mourn over his own sins.

All this is part of a divine plan in which the humble are full of purpose and influence while the proud are diminished. If you are looking for a role model who will enhance your reputation, the tax collector is one.

ᔕ ᔕ ᔕ

CIRCLE: Circle what is important.

REFLECT: Persuade yourself that *tax collector* is a noble and prized aspiration.

PRAY: Speak to the Lord: "God be merciful to me, a sinner."

TALK: Talk about God's understanding of true greatness.

DAY 14
WALKING WITH GOD

He has told you, O man, what is good;
and what does the Lord require of you
but to do justice, and to love kindness,
and to walk humbly with your God?
—*Micah 6:8*

My daughter was faced with a decision: Go to tennis practice, or go home with her father, who was insisting that she go to tennis practice. She paused for a moment. I could almost see her mind at work thinking, *If I go to tennis, I will hate it. I will be embarrassed by girls who have already been playing for years, and I am sure the coach will yell at me for not having a tennis outfit. Or I could go home with my dad. Whatever he does—stop my allowance, ground me for the year—it will not be worse than going to tennis.* I think she also believed that I would still love her. She chose to come home with me.

When you know God accurately, you don't walk away from him. Yes, he is awesome, and some have fallen down as though dead when they found themselves in his presence. But when people hear his voice, they want to come closer. Yes, hidden sins can make you want to run the other direction, but when you come to the point where you hate carrying around the guilt and shame and you actually hear what he says, you learn that God is downright excited when you stop running and glance in his direction. What's not to like?[8]

When you turn toward the Lord, he does not feed you gruel for the next month or roll his eyes. Instead, he walks with you. Today's passage rests on, "walk humbly with your God." Though God knows that every day you can be inattentive to his voice and so dishonor him, his desire from the beginning has been to walk with you, and in this walk, he promises to be with you and is committed to showing you his divine favor. In other words, he is good. The evidence is that he prefers to be with you—even if you have days when you are completely annoying.

God is great and over all the details of life, and humility makes more sense when you know that. God is good and loves you right now. Such love, freely given and clearly unearned, is certainly humbling. He does not ask you for blind trust or that you follow him in humility for no apparent reason. Instead, he invites you to know him. You learn, gradually, that he alone is trustworthy, great, and good.

It is a little easier to be under someone who you know loves you and wants the very best for you. The fear of the Lord, rightly understood, is amazement at his greatness *and* his holy love—an amazement that takes you a step in his direction, living under him.

Yet there is a deeper version of fear of the Lord. Humility walks *with* God. A walk is the ideal time for a conversation. He talks, *you listen*. You talk, *he listens*. On a walk, there are no distractions. A walk is just an undisturbed, unhurried afternoon with God. Humility has a chance to grow when you actually talk with your God.

Do justice, love kindness? We will turn soon to what humility looks like in living before other people. For now, know that these two virtues can only be sustained when you know his holy kindness and holy justice. For now, learn about your humble walk with the God who enjoys such things.

ဢ ဢ ဢ

CIRCLE: What is important here?

REFLECT: Imagine new ways for you to do justice and love kindness.

PRAY: Speak about the passage in your own words to the Lord. What do you want to say to the Lord as he walks with you?

TALK: Talk to one person.

DAY 15
A CHILD

At that time the disciples came to Jesus, saying, "Who is the greatest in the kingdom of heaven?" And calling to him a child, he put him in the midst of them and said, "Truly, I say to you, unless you turn and become like children, you will never enter the kingdom of heaven. Whoever humbles himself like this child is the greatest in the kingdom of heaven."
—*Matthew 18:1–4*

The comparison begins within only an hour or so after your first school day begins. Who is the smartest? Best looking? Best athlete? Who are the classroom elites? Who are the last people to be chosen in games? We can't help ourselves. Put us in a group and within ten minutes everyone has been assessed and assigned a number. Older cultures have formalized their class systems—*untouchables* or Brahmins. Newer cultures, like in the United States, have their informal systems—you have money and fame, or you don't. You are always evaluating and being evaluated. It is truly a wretched system with a history that reaches back even to Jesus's first disciples and beyond them to the beginning of time. Matthew records the disciples' question to Jesus—a barely veiled way of asking, "Which one of *us* is the greatest?" Or, "Am I the greatest?"

Jesus has been with them a while, so he has already pointed out how John the Baptist, who was penniless, homeless, and rejected, was among the greats (Matthew 11:11). We might imagine that Jesus would have absolutely freaked at the disciples' question, that he would have been amazed at the stupidity and arrogance of his followers, dismissed them, and gone in search of a more promising group. But since he is the God of unlimited patience, he simply took the opportunity to teach the way of true greatness. It seems out of reach, but we must aspire to be a trusting toddler before God. Our life depends on it.

Jesus is not saying that we are helpless and without wisdom or skills. He *is* saying that the game of who is up and who is down destroys community and friendship. It creates factions and is more interested in enhancing reputations than it is in love. In short, the prideful life that wants to get just a little higher, just a little bigger, is wicked. The secret of a young child's greatness lies in his neediness. He has no aspirations for greatness. He knows he needs help in everything. Without the right person in your corner, you can't get breakfast, have clean clothes, read a book, fend off a belligerent younger sister, or stand against the monsters that come at night. No fantasies of independence or self-reliance live here. When you need something, rather than devising a plan as you would if you were an orphaned street urchin, you cry out for your father. Jesus wants you to adopt as your own that simple cry of need to someone bigger than you who loves you.

Humility is poor and needy. You need what only God himself can give you. "Truly my soul finds rest in God" (Psalm 62:1 NIV). Your contentment and joy depend on it. You have the added benefit of knowing that Jesus always has eyes for those who perceive themselves of less consequence. In his kingdom, true greatness is always led by humility.

Do you ask for help with *anything*?
Do you ask people to pray for your spiritual needs?
Do you give thanks?
Do you listen?

A child does these things, at least on his or her better days. Jesus wants you to aspire to be the greatest.

CIRCLE: What is important in this devotional?

REFLECT: This one is not easy. "Stop being a child" is among the most disrespectful comments an adult could hear. Why would you say a child is great before God?

PRAY: Speak your thoughts of this to the Lord. Pray that he would make you into one of the greats.

TALK: Talk about how Jesus keeps giving us an understanding of life that is different from that of the world around us. What would it look like for you to aspire to be a child when you grow up?

DAY 16
THANKS

Oh give thanks to the Lord, for he is good;
for his steadfast love endures forever!
—1 Chronicles 16:34

The skill of humility is sharpened in three ordinary ways:

> *Worship:* May those who love your salvation say continually, "Great is the Lord!" (Psalm 40:16)
>
> *Confession:* Against you, you only, have I sinned. (Psalm 51:4).
>
> *Thanks:* Give thanks to the Lord, for his steadfast love endures forever. (2 Chronicles 20:21)

When even one of these essentials is part of your day, the world around you will notice a new strength, a heart more settled. The goal for today is to add more heft to your thanks. A man who thinks he is self-made and has paid his dues for the breaks he got along the way has no reason to express thanks. We, however, are not that man.

Our primary human teacher is the apostle Paul. He begins his letter to the Ephesians with a run-on sentence about his thanks and praise to the Father for the sacrificial love of Jesus Christ, the Son (1:3–14). And he is just getting started. Unlike our thanks for those things we can see, such as health, money, or fine weather, Paul prefers to list the blessings we have in Christ, which have immunity to the inevitable troubles we will experience in an hour or so. These are *spiritual* blessings, sealed to us by the Spirit. When our destinies are joined with Christ, our blessings are safely stored in him.

Here are a few of the gifts he identifies:

- He loved you when you didn't care about him.
- He chose you to be his. He has adopted you.
- You have been bought from the clutches of death.
- Sins, of course, have been forgiven, once and for all. Shame is on its way out.
- His grace is lavish to you today. God is not stingy.
- You have been elevated, in Christ, seated with him now. You are secure.
- None of this is through your own doing (Ephesians 2:8). Even your initial trust in Jesus was a gift to you from God.
- Today he has prepared "good works" for you (Ephesians 2:10), which means you have a reason to live. You are on the King's mission.
- His love is holy. It is more expansive than you can imagine, so you have the rest of eternity to grow in amazement.

You can add to the list above Jesus's reminder of reliable joy: "Rejoice that your names are written in heaven" (Luke 10:20). Today look for things that are certain but less easily seen (2 Corinthians 4:18).

The basic idea is to speak as much as you can to the Lord—about who he is, what he has done, and what he will do—and insert or end with "thank you." You could borrow words from psalmists, "thank you—your steadfast love for me endures forever. Who am I to be loved in such a way?" We can think of these words as the kind of sacrifices that God welcomes. They are voluntary public responses to the Lord that are both appropriate and pleasing to him. Pride cannot coexist with these thank offerings.

CIRCLE: What stands out? As a way to focus on the blessings Paul lists in Ephesians 1 and 2, add a Bible reference after each listed blessing above that doesn't include a reference.

REFLECT: Making a distinction between physical blessings and spiritual blessings is important. As a way to understand the contrast, write two different lists of thanks, one with three physical blessings (such as ways God has provided for you) and one with three spiritual blessings.

PRAY: Speak your thanks to the Lord.

TALK: Talk to someone about what you are learning. Share the spiritual thanksgiving list.

DAY 17
LISTEN

Listen diligently to me, and eat what is good,
and delight yourselves in rich food.
—*Isaiah 55:2*

Who comes to mind when you think about people who truly listen to the Lord? Consider these examples:

> I just spoke to a retired pastor. He made a passing comment that reminded me why I respect him. He said, "One of the best parts about retiring is that I get to learn from other preachers."
>
> Stan is on the transplant list. He is weak. He fatigues quickly. He is not among the world's influencers. Each morning he wakes up and forces himself to read Scripture. He would prefer to do nothing, but he overrides those thoughts and says, "Speak, Lord, your servant is listening." He reads until he can tell you something he has learned about God that causes him to give thanks.
>
> Leon got my attention during a sermon. I didn't know him well, but he was one of the few people who was taking notes. Lots of notes. A quiet young man, he came to church by himself. I met him after the service and have been his admirer ever since then.

To listen is to honor. Is there a preacher you respect? You listen and try to learn. If the sermon is recorded, you might listen again. Is there another preacher, less experienced or with a style you dislike? He is lesser. He preaches and your mind wanders off to what's for lunch. You also honor him by working at listening well. Your desire to listen is a gauge of humility.

The history of humanity warns us about how poorly we listen to the Lord. Over and over you read, "they did not listen. . . . they did not listen. . . . they did not listen." They didn't listen because they held other gods in higher regard. Look more closely and you see that they held *themselves* in higher regard. Our forefathers would go from god to god, depending on which one might give them what they wanted. Idolatry is not really about worship as much as it is about who will satisfy our personal desires. It is about our pride—the belief that nothing is above me and what I want. It turns out that idolatry is very familiar to us.

In response, the Lord intensifies his efforts to get your attention. The passage from Isaiah 55 is part of that effort. The repetition is a Hebrew way to add gravity to a word, and this is unprecedented repetition. The self-satisfied will not hear, but the needy will be all ears. Here is my paraphrase of some of his words:

> Come, everyone who is thirsty
> Come, for water
> Come, eat
> Come, without cost
> Listen
> Really listen, listen hard
> Turn your ear toward me
> Listen, you will receive the fullest of life (55:1–3)

How do you respond to him? Tell him.

How can we grow in being listeners of God? These two questions can help:

> *What are you learning about Jesus?* Always be prepared to tell someone. That is a way to be sure you are listening to the Spirit, whose mission is to reveal more of Jesus to you. Listening and learning is a sure sign that you are on this path of humility and wisdom.
>
> *What do you do because of Jesus and what he says to you?* That is a tougher one. True learning leads to action. Yesterday I was in a difficult conversation when I had the thought, *Okay, this is a good test for me. How do I follow Jesus now?* I mention this because the thought was refreshing and a bit too surprising. It is possible to be nice, listen, and control your temper with those things resulting more from what you want than from following Jesus. If what you do and say isn't in response to knowing Jesus, it has nothing to do with humility. All of life is to be a response to what Jesus has done for us.

Pride sticks its fingers in its ears. It doesn't need to listen, and it doesn't want to listen. *Humility listens to God.* That is how you can show him honor.

ೲ ೲ ೲ

CIRCLE: What do you hear in this devotional?

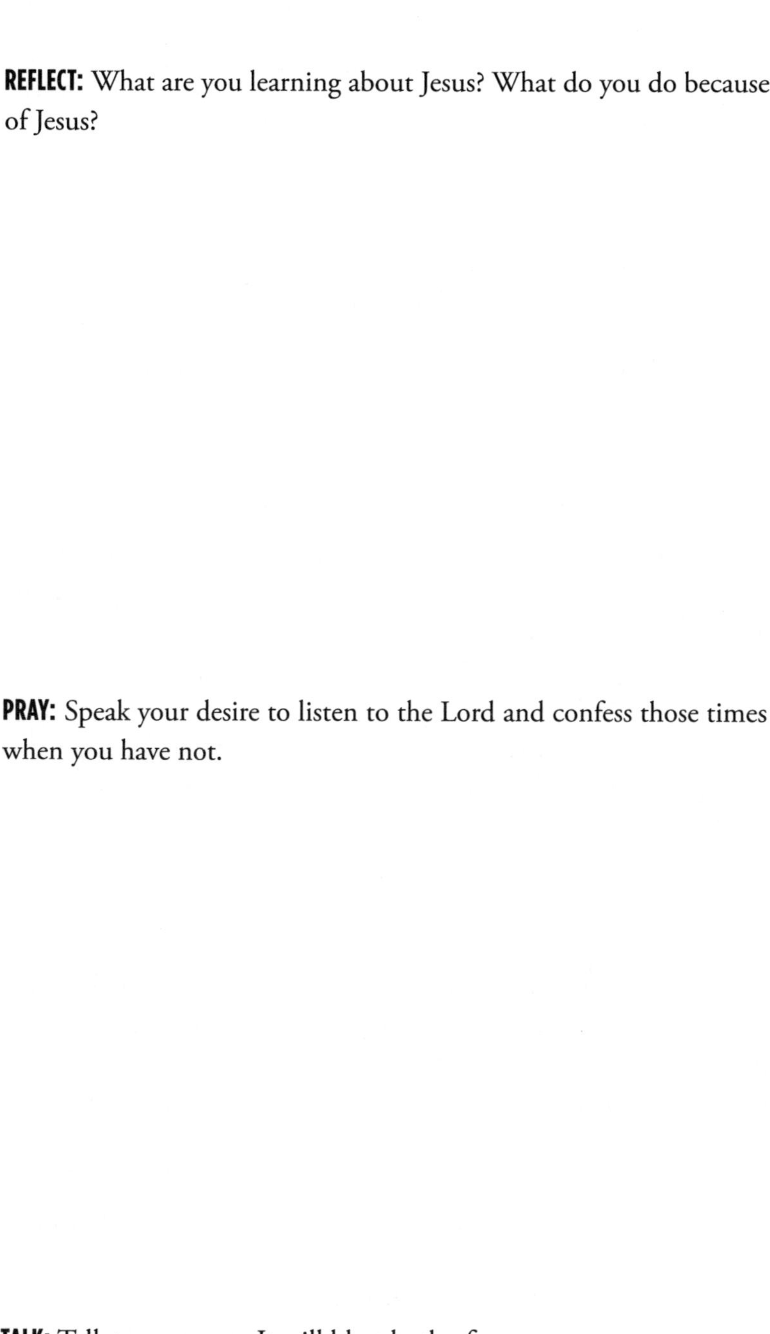

REFLECT: What are you learning about Jesus? What do you do because of Jesus?

PRAY: Speak your desire to listen to the Lord and confess those times when you have not.

TALK: Talk to someone. It will bless both of you.

DAY 18
RÉSUMÉS ON FIRE

Whatever gain I had, I counted as loss for the sake of Christ.
—*Philippians 3:7*

At first glance, this passage in Philippians 3 seems to be a plea to embrace your inner donkey or practice being a worm. But if you look closer, you will see that it is a radical path that allows you to *rise above* the need for respect and reputation that both runs and ruins many lives.

The apostle Paul invites you to update your personal résumé. It could be the actual résumé you use to get job interviews, but it also includes unique personal achievements and abilities—fitness, sport, gaming, eating, memory, math. Now consider those things that are of greatest value to you. Some might not even receive mention. For example, a colleague of mine was speaking to a large group when, without warning, he couldn't find words. A few seconds later, he couldn't compose clear thoughts. I remember being struck by his casualness (the problem was transient) when he later told me that in his final moments of clarity, he reflected, "Since my job requires that I think and talk, this could be a problem." Thinking and talking were not on his résumé, but they were essential to it. Now imagine one prized attribute after another being scrubbed. When would you begin to really feel that loss? When would you finally feel like there is no point in living?

The apostle Paul lived out this exercise. He built a reputation, and then he cast off everything that built it. When he tells his story, he first reviews those things that made him somebody: "If anyone else thinks he has reason for confidence in the flesh, I have more: circumcised on the eighth day, of the people of Israel, of the tribe of Benjamin, a Hebrew of Hebrews; as to the law, a Pharisee; as to zeal, a persecutor of the church; as to righteousness under the law, blameless" (Philippians 3:4–6). This is a heady list for that era. It is more than enough for him to feel pretty good about himself and to look down on lesser people.

Then he met Jesus. In a moment, he began revising his story. Every Jew suddenly considered him no better than a Gentile dog, and Paul was thrilled—not so much with the hatred of his people but because he had gained Christ. He knew that he could not have both pride in his own achievements and pride in being tied to the Son of God. One earned the praise of other men; the other gave him Jesus. He was so adamant that nothing would get in the way of having Christ's righteousness alone that, just in case the old sources of pride would sneak in and puff him up, he threw them away as though they were all worthy of disdain. In his calculations, he lost nothing and gained everything.

Today there are indeed men and women who have followed Jesus and lost everything. It's likely that you are not among them. As a result, you can build your life on some mix of what you do well and what Christ has done for you. You might think that this would leave a mix of pride and humility, but that's not how it works. When we rest in *anything* apart from Christ, that desire becomes our idol, and as with all idols, God plus any idol is simply idolatry.

If we are asked to identify the primary hazards of daily life, we would probably think of pain, failure, and loss of health, money, relationships, or reputation. But Paul disagrees. These have their challenges, but they are not the biggest threats. *Our perceived successes pose the greatest danger*. Our human tendency is to find something we have done to prop up our identity. For that, we don't need an endless résumé, though we might prefer one. We will usually settle for something that is just a bit more impressive than some achievement on someone else's résumé.

Paul invites you to burn your résumé now rather than watch it combust on the day you die (1 Peter 1:7). It turns out that by following Jesus you cast off sins, regrets, shame, *and* your good works. Only then can you know something—Someone—of surpassing worth and gain an inheritance that will survive the refiner's fire.

ꕥ ꕥ ꕥ

CIRCLE: Lots to circle here. What seems important?

REFLECT: What parts of your résumé would be better if they were thrown in the fire? Look for those that bolster how you hope to be seen by the world. Start your list.

PRAY: Talk to Jesus about this. Tell him what needs to burn and how you want your true résumé to have his name written all over it.

TALK: Success is the greatest danger. That is worth talking about with someone.

DAY 19

WHO AM I?

Then King David went in and sat before the Lord and said, "Who am I, O Lord God, and what is my house, that you have brought me thus far?"

—2 Samuel 7:18; 1 Chronicles 17:16

"Who am I?" has different meanings. One has to do with personal identity: "I am a teacher, a member of my local church." Another is a response to a great gift: "I don't deserve this," "You shouldn't have," or, "Who am I to receive this?" Today, consider again the place that thanks has in your heart.

Before David became king of Israel, he was the overlooked runt of the litter. He was a wandering shepherd in a low-status position when the Lord called him to shepherd the people. Not only that, the prophet Nathan also revealed that David's line of kings would be eternal. From his line, the Messiah himself would come and rule over the earth (2 Samuel 7:12–13). In response, David said, "Who am I?" He was humbled by such a great gift.

You have also been brought into that eternal kingdom. The apostle Paul reminds you again and again that you are "in Christ" and all that is his is now yours. You are in David's lineage and you have reason to repeat his exact words. Even more, you have received what David could not imagine. You know the eternal King, and his Spirit dwells in you.

The challenge is that your days don't feel that impressive. Life is hard and full of trouble. Bills have to be paid. You have to reckon with a less-than-promising financial future. Yes, God's love for you is nice, but sometimes it carries the same weight as your mother's love, which doesn't reach into the hard details of life. Thoughts about an eternal kingdom seem like a luxury for those who can get their head above the endless demands of the present.

The hardships in your life are real, but they are an incomplete picture of your life. David had endless wars with enemies on his borders and in his own house, but he stopped to look in awe at his Lord. And although Paul faced death and shame every day, he reminds you, "Thanks be to God for his inexpressible gift!" (2 Corinthians 9:15). His thankfulness carried more weight in his life than his pain. In other words, in spite of any hardships, your faith and humility—your relationship with God—depend on your ability to say to the Lord, "Who am I?"

> *Who am I?* I was stone-cold dead before Jesus made me alive. I was without Jesus, the Spirit's presence, and left on my own in a world where death would declare everything about my life useless.
>
> *Who am I?* While I have been indifferent and unfaithful, Jesus is faithful to me.
>
> *Who am I?* I was chosen by God from before the foundations of the world.
>
> *Who am I?* I am known by God. Seen. Cared for.
>
> *Who am I?* I know God, and he loves me with steadfast love.

So what gifts have you received? God's steadfast love is a fine thing, but it must move you toward God. Search out any remnant of "I deserve," because it is a killer to faith and life. Then look for those spiritual realities you can't see.

ꟷ ꟷ ꟷ

CIRCLE: What stands out to you today?

REFLECT: This presses you again for a quick list of spiritual blessings—certain and eternal. Review your reflection from Day 16, and add more. What has Jesus done for you? Only those things that excite your soul count.

PRAY: "Who am I that you would remember me?" Use that question as you recount God's blessings.

TALK: You could tell someone why you give thanks today.

DAY 20
A SERVANT

Paul, a servant of Christ Jesus.
—Romans 1:1

James, a servant of God and of the Lord Jesus Christ.
—James 1:1

Simeon Peter, a servant and apostle of Jesus Christ.
—2 Peter 1:1

In the Bible, *servant* is a carefully guarded and prized identity, never conferred on just anyone. The Lord called Abraham and Moses "my servant" (Genesis 26:24; Exodus 14:31). They were part of a small, elite group. Joshua, the flawless leader who followed Moses, had not quite measured up, at least not yet: "After the death of Moses, *the servant of the LORD*, the Lord said to Joshua *the son of Nun* . . ." (Joshua 1:1, emphasis added). Only much later, after years of faithful service, Joshua was highly honored: "After these things Joshua the son of Nun, *the servant of the LORD*, died, being 110 years old (Joshua 24:29, emphasis added). Joshua made it. King David would follow in receiving the honored designation (2 Samuel 3:18).

The title of *servant* was restricted for a reason. It was being held for The Servant, who was foretold by the prophet Isaiah and would astound the world by serving his people—even offering his life for their own. A title is made great by those who possessed that title before you, and Jesus is the true and first Servant.

In Isaiah's four Servant Songs, Jesus is clearly revealed as the true Servant hundreds of years before he appeared. The first song identifies his gentleness—"a faintly burning wick he will not quench" (Isaiah

42:3), yet he alone will bring justice to the nations. The second song proclaims that his service will bless the nations in such a way that joy breaks out and comfort and compassion are freely given (49:1–13). The third song takes a hard turn from that joy when the servant submits to his Father and endures shame and disgrace (50:4–9). The fourth draws together the themes of his crushing death, the strength of a victor, and sublime joy (52:13–53:12). From the beginning, the Servant's mission was summed up in the words, "he bore the sin of many" (53:12).

As we try to be faithful to Scripture's discussion about humility, we know that humility is first before God, and it begins with being served by our humble God. "For even the Son of Man came not to be served but to serve, and to give his life as a ransom for many" (Mark 10:45). This is why the first disciples of Jesus prized the designation *servant* as among their most honored identities. Jesus is The Servant, and they were given the honor of taking on his résumé and walking as he walked.

Jesus wants the image of him washing the disciples' feet and your own to stay in your mind (John 13). As he takes the role of your servant, he is doing much more than washing smelly feet. The water symbolizes the daily cleansing that washes the sinful debris of the day. Remember how the Father does not forget the injustices done against us? That also means that he is certainly aware of the injustices we have perpetrated. Much happened when you put your trust in Jesus rather than in yourself. Jesus has already appeared on your behalf before the Judge of the world. The Father accepts Jesus as your substitute. His life for yours. Now you are closely identified with him and what he has done.

This means that you also receive Jesus's righteousness and holiness—his cleanness. So Jesus speaks to you the words he spoke to Peter: "The one who has bathed does not need to wash, except for his feet, but is completely clean" (John 13:10). You are acceptable before the Father because you have been cleansed. The little washings Jesus gives your feet are reminders that he has already washed your body and soul, making you always presentable before God, never rejected, and given new mercy every morning. The big cleansing makes an enemy into a son and heir; the smaller cleansings prepare you each day so that your sins do not leave you timid before your Father.

The Son has made you a son. The Servant has brought you into his proud lineage. Like a new CEO who follows the most successful and revered CEO in company history, you are honored yet a little concerned that you will single-handedly bring down the prestige of the position. This position, however, is different from most. Jesus is with you now, and his Spirit will raise your game in a way that makes you worthy of the title *servant*. Abraham, Moses, and David are pleased to include you as one whom God calls "my servant."

∽ ∽ ∽

CIRCLE: What do you want to remember here?

REFLECT: Add the highly honored title "my servant" to your personal résumé. How do you hope to wear that honor today?

PRAY: Talk to the Lord about this. What do you need from him in order to serve him faithfully?

TALK: Talk to a brother about what you are learning.

DAY 21
THE HUMBLE GOD

Do nothing from selfish ambition or conceit, but in humility count others more significant than yourselves. Let each of you look not only to his own interests, but also to the interests of others. Have this mind among yourselves, which is yours in Christ Jesus, who, though he was in the form of God, did not count equality with God a thing to be grasped, but emptied himself, by taking the form of a servant.

—Philippians 2:3–7

"We are adults. We can do anything we want." I use that justification with my wife when I grab a second dessert, head to the beach with her on a beautiful day while leaving a few responsibilities behind, or announce an impromptu breakfast run. I am not breaking any laws, and I am not quite serious when I say those words, but you recognize what lurks in the heart. I feel free when I have no one telling me what to do. The phrase in Genesis summarizes this feeling: "You will be like God" (Genesis 3:5). That is a temptation few humans can resist.

In contrast, Jesus was both God and the true, fully alive, human. He lived his entire life on earth in obedience to the Father. He was *The* Suffering Servant. "Not my will" was his life verse. But the idea of being a servant takes some getting used to for us. Ask me to do something and I might do it; *tell* me to do something and I will start looking for ways to get out from under your authority, assuming you have some authority to demand such things. Jesus, however, was not scared off by obedience. He welcomed it. He gave up his authority and lived to please his Father (John 5:30). He added, "My teaching is not mine, but his who sent me" (John 7:16).

Jesus came by humility naturally. The triune God doesn't quarrel over who is top dog or who possesses what. Sometimes it can seem like the Father has the top billing, but the truth is that the Father, Son, and Spirit share in a mission to bring people into himself and cover the earth with the glory of God. Each of the triune persons engages in honoring the other. The key to all this is the love shared between the Father, Son, and Spirit.

It is painful to obey someone you don't like. That is hard to sustain. But when you love someone, you ask, "How can I help?" or, "What would you like me to do for you today?" When you love someone, you might even take their wardrobe suggestions.

Jesus loves the Father, so obedience was his deep desire. Now he leads us all by grounding obedience in love.

> If you love me, you will keep my commandments. (John 14:15)

> For this is the love of God, that we keep his commandments. And his commandments are not burdensome. (1 John 5:3)

Humility means that you walk with God, dependent on him, in the fear of the Lord, with a teachable heart. The fear of the Lord is a fine way to begin this walk. God alone is God, and you are controlled by him rather than your own desires. Awe is a fine thing. Yet fear is never separated from love. "The eye of the LORD is on those who *fear* him, on those who hope in his steadfast *love*" (Psalm 33:18, emphasis added). The words are used interchangeably. *Fear* accents that the person you love is stunning.

The pattern is becoming clear. The passage begins with our own humility or lack of it, but it aims for something even more important—the humility of Jesus in his care for you. Then it gets to a question: "Do you love me?" Jesus asked Peter this question after Peter's three denials of knowing him. This is the question he asks you. If you don't respond, he is happy to ask you again and again, until you answer.

ℰ ℰ ℰ

CIRCLE: What do you want to remember today?

REFLECT: Love for God is what makes humility sweet. How does that work in your life? Imagine how it could work.

PRAY: Speak to him. Answer him as he asks, "Do you love me?" Tell him. Do you love him poorly but want to love him more? Tell him.

TALK: Do you want to ask a friend to pray for you?

DAY 22
THE FEEL OF HUMILITY

From that time Jesus began to show his disciples that he must go to Jerusalem and suffer many things from the elders and chief priests and scribes, and be killed, and on the third day be raised. . . . Then Jesus told his disciples, "If anyone would come after me, let him deny himself and take up his cross and follow me."
—Matthew 16:21, 24

You would think that humility would feel natural. We are all under someone or something—laws, magistrates, taxes, and even church leaders. And God is over us and over them. The life and gifts we have are from him. We have no reason to boast. Pride, delusions of independence, and arrogance are old instincts. But humility was not natural for Jesus's disciples—that is, until things changed.

The disciples were transformed in a moment. They witnessed the crucifixion and resurrection, and the Spirit of Christ came on them to stay. The path in front of them was the way of a humble servant, and they were overjoyed. It was humanity as we were always intended to be. It was the abundant life. Humility is not the path of always getting lower. Instead, it lives dependent on the God of life. Once we get the knack of it, it is natural and good.

Think for a moment about what having humility before God feels like. We want to be sure we are headed in a right and good direction. Consider the following list:

- You are glad these devotions started off with *humility before God.*

- You don't have to hide that you are reading this book.
- You talk to God more often. Prayer is a gauge for humility.
- You actually ask God for help. A warning: When you ask God, you will also more naturally ask for help and prayer from other people. Your prayer requests will be more vulnerable and honest.
- You have given thanks to the Lord for things you see and don't see. This will also overflow into the gratitude you express for others.
- You can feel inadequate and be mostly okay with it. Or at least you can talk to Jesus about it.
- You see the possibilities for being more settled in who you are and who you are not. You are almost okay with the idea of not being somebody special.
- You listen more carefully to sermons.
- You sing a little louder during worship.
- You can identify one area of sin that the Spirit has shown you, and you think that is a good thing.
- You have said something to the Lord about your troubles and hardships.
- If you are married, your wife is glad that you are reading this.

Your opinion of what humility looks like has changed so that you can describe it in a way that captures its goodness. Do any of these descriptions ring true?

> Humility means that you live before God alone, dependent on him, honoring him, fearing him, loving him, listening to him. You wake up in the morning, throw away your résumé—again—and say, "Your will be done." You reject the old project of personal reputation and status. You are not your own. You belong to another, and you couldn't be more pleased.

> Humility is neediness before God, faith in Christ, submission to the Lord, and crying over your sins. You identify with the tax collector, a servant, and a child. They are among your heroes.
>
> Humility says aloud, "I am not worthy. Who am I? Against you I have sinned. You are holy in your greatness and goodness. Thank you. I trust you. I love you." Each word is a response to your God who died for you in Christ so that you could live with him.

This takes us full circle—when we take on humility, God lifts us up (James 4:10). Next let's consider what humility looks like before other people.

ᔕ ᔕ ᔕ

CIRCLE: Does anything surprise you here?

REFLECT: What is your version of a summary of where we are?

PRAY: Pray for what you want to see in your life.

TALK: Talk to someone about what you have circled.

HUMILITY BEFORE OTHERS

Humility is first humility before God.
Humility before God is then worked out in your relationships,
as it serves God's purpose of bringing people together in Christ.

DAY 23

AS THE KING, SO THE PEOPLE

I therefore, a prisoner for the Lord, urge you to walk in a manner worthy of the calling to which you have been called, with all humility and gentleness, with patience, bearing with one another in love, eager to maintain the unity of the Spirit in the bond of peace.
—*Ephesians 4:1–3*

Humility and gentleness lead the way. Patience and love follow. In Ephesians, Paul is repeating the words that Jesus uses of himself: "humble" and "gentle" (Matthew 11:29 NIV). Paul has already told you that your life in Christ "is not your own doing"—none of it, not one bit (Ephesians 2:8). It is all from Jesus, and you simply receive it by faith. So, as Paul turns from life in Christ to life with each other, you are not surprised when he begins "with all humility and gentleness." That is suitable for those who received a great gift.

As the King walks, so do the people. He walked before us in humility and gentleness, so we do the same. This is God's way. Consider when Moses was told to bring water from a rock on two occasions. In the first, the people were quarreling and "tested the Lord by saying, 'Is the Lord among us or not?'" (Exodus 17:7). This is a serious and arrogant crime against the Lord. Moses was told to strike the rock in a similar way to how he struck the Nile, which suggests that it was a rebuke to the people (17:5). In other words, Moses did what God asked in a way that imitated God.

The second time God brought water from a rock, the people quarreled with Moses but also called themselves "the assembly of the Lord" (Numbers 20:4). This was a step in the right direction. This time the Lord told Moses to *speak* to the rock. God's wrath is absent. Instead, *Moses* is angry. He strikes the rock twice as his way to express *his* wrath. In doing this, he misrepresents the Lord to the people, which is the reason he was denied entry to the land God promised: "because you did not treat me as holy in the midst of the people of Israel. For you shall see the land before you, but you shall not go there" (Deuteronomy 32:51–52). Keep your eyes on Jesus, and humility and gentleness will be natural. Other people's actions and opinions will not carry the weight they once did.

Humility is submission to God. So as you go through your days in humility with God—needing him, resting in him, eager to hear his words, and eager to talk with him—this attitude goes out into the street in the hopes that it will be on display in your relationships in ways that are simple and honoring to the God who serves you. Humility is to walk *with* the Servant-King, *like* the Servant-King, in the *power* of the Servant-King, for the good of others and the unity of God's people.

Gentleness assumes that you have strength and are pleased to restrain it so that it suits the occasion. It contrasts with bullying and using manipulation and anger to get your way. It contrasts with our tendency to fight dirty when we think the other person started it, and to say, "Well, if that's the way you want to play, I can play that way too." Gentleness is strength within wise limits. It prefers careful reflection in the face of provocative acts, rather than reacting on first impulse. It considers how to surprise those who expected you to take up arms, as Christ still surprises you with his gentleness in the face of your orneriness.

Then Paul adds patience and love as close companions of humility and gentleness. *Patience can put up with the thoughtless or rude behaviors of others.* God remains patient with you, and you hope to pass his patience on to others. Are you patient with that person who always seems to talk about himself? When you share something that happened in your week, he shares something bigger and more dramatic. Patience might recognize that people who feel small often try to take up more conversational space, and it could listen and even enjoy the person's story before considering how to move the conversation to even more important matters: "Tell me, what are you learning these days?" "What has been most important in your life?" How should we pray for that hard relationship at work?"

The love Paul described is best explained by a novelist who dedicated his book to his two daughters. He explained that he might never have known love apart from them. Unlike so much marital love that can run hot and cold depending on how loveable a spouse can be at any moment, children open up a new world in which you are happy to serve them even when you get nothing in return. *You love them more than you need to be loved by them*, and that takes you to a pinnacle of human existence, which means it takes you into humility.

So begins your walk with God *and* with people. Your mission is not simply to be nice. Instead, we are part of a much larger project of building a united people in a fragmented world, and it is done in humility and gentleness.

ꕥ ꕥ ꕥ

CIRCLE: What catches your attention in this discussion? The story of Moses is sobering.

REFLECT: How would you describe gentleness? Be sure to include how it imitates the gentleness of Jesus toward you. When have you not been gentle?

PRAY: Pray Ephesians 4:1–3.

TALK: Do you need to confess times when you were not gentle?

DAY 24
CONFESSING SIN

If you are offering your gift at the altar and there remember that your brother has something against you, leave your gift there before the altar and go. First be reconciled to your brother, and then come and offer your gift.
—*Matthew 5:23–24*

After I came to know Jesus, I didn't think I sinned—at least not that much. I never quite saw how my selfishness and pride knew no bounds. Then I got married. Within four days, I was agreeing with the apostle Paul: "Wretched man that I am! Who will deliver me from this body of death?" (Romans 7:24). I first blamed my wife for this sudden downhill course. After all, I had been a decent guy before. The only thing in my life that had changed was her presence.

But that kind of rationalization can be difficult to sustain in the face of the evidence. As I noticed that I wasn't always the good guy I had thought I was, the Spirit of God set me off on a slow, meandering path on which I would gradually learn about confessing sin. Even if you wander off this path of confession occasionally, it is still the most direct path to humility. I hope you learn to love it. What pleases God on our walk with him? "The sacrifices of God are a broken spirit; a broken and contrite heart, O God, you will not despise" (Psalm 51:17).

Notice where the Spirit convicts you of sin. You know it is the Spirit when conviction comes with gentleness and does not list the hundred or so sins that could easily be identified. Confess those things the Spirit convicts you of. Confess sins that *you do*—anger, complaining, jealousy, and destructive words—and confess what *you don't do*—love God and neighbor deeply from the heart. Say with the psalmist, "As for me, I am poor and needy, but the Lord takes thought for me" (Psalm 40:17).

Confession follows the same pattern as humility—first we confess to the Lord, and then we confess to people we have offended. The overwhelming majority of Scripture passages about confession and forgiveness guide us toward confession before God, rather than people. Confession remains the shortest path to fruitful humility.

Once you are accustomed to confessing your sins to the Lord, it will be a small step to confess your sin to the person you offended. If this is new, it will be the hardest and best thing you have done, and there is no better time than the present. Who have you sinned against? Who comes to mind? If you live with someone, that person is a likely candidate.

Keep in mind two pieces of wisdom:

> Don't confess your private sins against another person. If you cursed them in your heart and not to their face, confess that to the Lord. (But chances are you have also sinned against them in words or deeds that *have* been public.)
>
> Don't be tricked into believing that you simply reacted to the other person's sin: "She started it," or "What he did was much worse." Your sin is your sin, so own it.

God's words have urgency when we have sinned against other people. Reconcile now. But consider what you will say. This is not a game of hot potato in which you pass the responsibility from yourself ("Please forgive me") to the other person ("Now you have to forgive me"). Sin damages people. You know this because you yourself have been damaged by sin. Confession is part of a larger process of reconciling and rebuilding. The critical issue now is that you ask forgiveness, specifically, with sincerity, willing to listen to the consequences it had on the other person, and looking to redouble the battle against that sin. For instance, "I have been thinking about what I said. I was so wrong to have said that. I am so sorry. Would you forgive me?"

Humility is strength. Its words of confession might have the greatest impact you could ever have on another person. Imagine a church in which we could quickly confess our sins against each other.

ꕤ ꕤ ꕤ

CIRCLE: This is important. What stands out to you most in this devotion?

REFLECT: Who comes to mind? What will you say to that person? When will you talk to that person? If you are reluctant, talk to a friend about it. If you can't think of anyone you have damaged, don't forget about your children. If you have children, you have sinned against them. If nothing comes to mind, how would you like a family member or friend to pray for you?

PRAY: Your sins against others are first against God. Work this through. Talk to him. Why is your sin against another person against him? Psalm 51 can help you with words.

TALK: Easier to act now than later.

DAY 25

BEING "RIGHT"

If I speak in the tongues of men and of angels, but have not love, I am a noisy gong or a clanging cymbal. And if I have prophetic powers, and understand all mysteries and all knowledge, and if I have all faith, so as to remove mountains, but have not love, I am nothing.

—1 Corinthians 13:1–2

I hate marital tension, especially during a night out or on a vacation. I realize that no time is convenient for it, but still, I would prefer that it didn't intrude into times that are officially designated for rest and peace.

My wife and I were on a short holiday at the beach. I was doing some very spiritual reading—Spurgeon or some other reliable theologian—and she said something. I have no recollection of what it was, but it got me thinking, *What she is saying is not true.* I seemed to remember that she had said things like that before. *This time I am going to help her. I am going to help her see that she is wrong.*

My reasoning was sound. My choice of reading material assured me that I was a discerning human being—no frivolous beach novels here—so my judgment was keen from the start. I was doing this for *her,* and hard things done with the heart of a servant are so noble. Without a hint of anger, I approached the situation calmly, matter-of-factly. I didn't want to provoke her or put her on the defensive. So I was a little surprised when she didn't receive it well. I don't remember the details of the next hour or two, but I do remember she said we were going to have to "agree to disagree," which had never been helpful for us in the past.

As we walked together to the beach the next day in a relationship that was a bit chilly, maybe even silent, a simple truth broke through. This is one of the beauties of Scripture—it gives the way of wisdom and makes it available to anyone with ears to hear. Expect a simple question to be your means of deliverance.

Did I love?

This question is stamped all over Scripture, and yet I missed it. *Being right* was a deceptive cover. It felt orthodox. I felt manly and leader-like. I thought I was standing for the truth. But it was *my truth* that concerned me, not the truth about Jesus. Once I was unmasked as an irritatingly loud gong, the truth was clear: I did *not* love.

I immediately asked forgiveness. I might have even gotten on my knees, which I commend as a great way to pray, ask forgiveness, and ask someone to marry you. Two things happened: First, peace rushed in as she easily forgave. Second, I completely forgot what I was so right about. A vacation recovered, and a relationship deepened and improved.

These events are etched in my conscience and leave me afraid of the deceptive nature of sin. But that fear is more than counterbalanced by the knowledge that the Spirit loves us by bringing our hearts into the light in the gentlest of ways. Self-deception will have to wait for another day.

Does this mean that love does not raise any concerns? No. Humility is not silence. It is, however, quick to listen.

ɞ ɞ ɞ

CIRCLE: What stands out to you?

REFLECT: Pride can be so certain. That should arouse our suspicion because certainty doesn't listen. In that initial conversation, how could I have raised my questions with my wife?

PRAY: Hear the Spirit's question: *Did you love?* How do you answer him?

You could also pray Paul's prayer for us, "that your love may abound more and more, with knowledge and all discernment, so that you may approve what is excellent" (Philippians 1:9–10).

TALK: This one might include a confession to someone.

DAY 26
COME AND DIE

And he [Jesus] said to all, "If anyone would come after me, let him deny himself and take up his cross daily and follow me. For whoever would save his life will lose it, but whoever loses his life for my sake will save it."
—*Luke 9:23–24*

Jesus's admonition to deny yourself and take up your cross and follow him are not new to you. You hear them in other familiar texts, such as, "Not my will, but yours, be done" (Luke 22:42). Or, "You are not your own, for you were bought with a price" (1 Corinthians 6:19–20). But these verses in Luke grab you like no other. Jesus works to get your attention by saying, "Follow me and die."

Dying with Jesus. When Jesus speaks these words to his disciples, he is talking about actual death. Will you follow the Crucified One into death? For the disciples, this meant a physical death that was most likely a Roman crucifixion or something just as painful. For most of us, it will mean other ways to die. To "take up your cross" is to want your death to glorify God (John 21:19). Can you trust him through dementia, ALS, or cancer?

At this time, I have a family member who has somewhere between three days and three weeks to live. He is too weak to do anything—too weak to sit up, lift a fork, or go to the toilet. He is dependent on other people for everything. And he is following Jesus into this death. So it is no surprise that life is more obvious in him. He is kinder, grateful for those who clean him, funnier because he doesn't take himself as seriously as he once did, and eager to repair broken relationships from conflicts that once seemed so big but are now barely remembered. His old pride has lost its grip, and a fuller—more alive—human is taking his place.

Dietrich Bonhoeffer walked the same path. He said, "When Christ calls a man, he bids him come and die."[9] By all accounts, he walked that path with courage, faith that battled hard, and humility.

Living with Jesus by dying. On this path of humility with Jesus Christ, you walk with him even if that means death. During that walk, you daily put to death the remnants of your sinful desires. You are already on that path as you say, "Your will be done." The apostle Paul ran with this. He wrote in Galatians, "Those who belong to Christ Jesus have crucified the flesh with its passions and desires" (5:24), and then, "far be it from me to boast except in the cross of our Lord Jesus Christ, by which the world has been crucified to me, and I to the world" (6:14).

So what needs to die? What are you crucifying? What interferes with your love for Jesus and your love for other people? Paul pushes these questions into everyday life, where pride quietly stalks. Look for pride where you judge others, not so much because they are in clear disobedience, but because you believe you are more right than they (Romans 14:1–12). It could be your judgment about worship styles, dress, parenting, lateness, diet, weight . . . anything that makes you a little more right than someone else. Paul asks who you really live for—the Lord or yourself (Romans 14:8)? He concludes, "each of us will give an account *of himself* to God" (14:12, emphasis added).

It all sounds quite intense, and it is sobering. But it is also a normal part of any close relationship. To be close to another, you lay down your life for them. Think about marriage. When you marry, you give up plenty. You suddenly live for another, not simply for yourself. Yet when the marriage is good, it feels like your life is so much richer. You have not given up a thing, but you have gained so much more.

Here is the good life. Jesus said, "It is written, 'Man shall not live by bread alone, but by every word that comes from the mouth of God'" (Matthew 4:4). This is the crucified life. This is what you have been looking for.

ↀ ↀ ↀ

CIRCLE: What do you hear most clearly?

REFLECT: Put "come and die" in your own words. What needs to die?

PRAY: When Jesus calls you to a path, he gives you grace to live that path. What do you want to say to him? What do you want to ask for? You can also confess, "I do not live by bread alone, but by every word that comes from the mouth of God."

TALK: The crucified life is worth talking about.

DAY 27
PSALM 46

The LORD of hosts is with us;
the God of Jacob is our fortress.
—Psalm 46:7

The intensity of Jesus's words to "come and die" now turns to the psalms and their specialty in "unselfing."[10] They are prayers that might begin with our terrible circumstances or our horrible hearts, but then take us outside of ourselves to our Holy God, making life better. You are no longer the center of the universe. Ah, imagine. A heart less cluttered with yourself. Instead, there is room for God and other people.

A dear friend had just been taken back to his hospital room after a long and difficult surgery. When he regained consciousness in his hospital room, pain overwhelmed him, and he could only repeat one phrase: "God is a very present help in trouble." What a fine instinct for our souls.

Enter Psalm 46. Come prepared with two things. First, have in mind a troubling circumstance that can be described as though the earth itself is melting beneath you. Second, see that the psalm is by Jesus and about him, and he invites you to share in his words. Circle what seems especially important. Look for a verse that comes close to what is in your own soul. Notice the unselfing as it happens.

Jesus—Jesus Christ and him crucified—is our refuge and strength,
a very present help in trouble.

Therefore we will not fear though the earth give way,
though the mountains be moved into the heart of the sea,
though its waters roar and foam,
because his Spirit is with us. *Selah*
There is a river whose streams make glad the city of God,
his holy habitation, which is now ours.
Jesus is the enthroned King in the midst of her; she shall not be moved;
He will help her when morning dawns.
Power is the Lord's. The nations rage, the kingdoms totter;
he utters his voice, the earth melts.
Jesus, the Lord of mighty armies, is with us;
Jesus, the God even of Jacob (who was a con and a deceiver) is our fortress. *Selah* (vv. 1–7, author paraphrase)

This final verse brings you to a place of rest in the Lord. Now the unselfing begins in earnest. Your attention moves beyond yourself. You think of other people and invite them to know God.

Come, behold the works of the Lord Jesus,
How, through weakness and his death on a cross, he is subduing the earth.
He has brought peace between God and his people.
It is a peace that make wars cease
to the end of the earth. (46:8–9, author paraphrase)

The Lord himself hears your words, and he is pleased by them. Now he speaks.

Be still, and know that I, Jesus the King, am the Mighty God.
I will be exalted among the nations,
I will be exalted in the earth!
The Devil's reign over death is ended. (46:10, author paraphrase)

In response, you repeat the refrain, but with more confidence.

The Lord Jesus, who leads his armies, is with me;
the Lord Jesus, who is pleased to say that he is Jacob's God,
is my fortress. *Selah* (46:11, author paraphrase)

ᘓᘒ ᘓᘒ ᘓᘒ

CIRCLE: What was good for your soul?

REFLECT: Why was it good for your soul? Did any unselfing happen?

PRAY: Speak or write out the psalm again, changing it to a more personal prayer.

TALK: Psalms are intended to be public. Read part of it aloud with someone.

DAY 28
ANGER

What causes quarrels and what causes fights among you?
Is it not this, that your passions are at war within you?
You desire and do not have, so you murder.
—James 4:1–2

The angry person is the weakest of all (Proverbs 25:28). "You *made* me angry." Anger is always someone else's fault, and the angry person cannot even control himself. So fragile. With the smallest provocation, an angry person explodes. Yet we are all friends with anger, and we feel strong when we wield it. But the angrier we are—the more right we believe our cause—the more we morph into a blind fool. Anger is the emblem of arrogant pride. Its motto is "I want!" Anger is unfamiliar with "your [God's] will be done" (Matthew 6:10). It can only be countered by those who are willing to "mourn and weep" and "humble yourselves before the Lord" (James 4:9–10). These are ways that the Lord says, "Come and die." This is the way to true strength—God's strength.

Since you will be blind to your anger, even though other people are *not* blind to it, keep track of its disguises. Murder, violence, hatred, yelling, arguing, cursing, conflict, blame, revenge, irritability, jealousy, slander, gossip, sarcasm, grumbling and bad complaining, withdrawal and silence, and even feeling happy about the struggles of others. As a fellow human being, you have a problem with anger.

Jesus himself is angry when Pharisees try to prohibit him from healing a man with a withered hand (Mark 3:5), when money-changers interfere with Gentile worship (John 2:13–17), and when his disciples try to fence him from little children (Mark 10:14). Yet notice this: He is never angry when sin is directed against him personally, but only when it is used to oppress others. And he never takes independent, vigilante-style action. Instead, "When he was reviled, he did not revile in return; when he suffered, he did not threaten, but continued entrusting himself to him who judges justly" (1 Peter 2:23). So don't think your anger or the anger of other people is *holy* anger. Jesus's holy anger is patient, always listens, seeks to reason you back to reality, and is quick to forgive. If you can't say those things about your anger, then it's definitely not like God's holy anger.

The most chilling thing about your anger is its connection to the Devil. The Devil is an angry murderer (John 8:44, Ephesians 4:26–27). Our anger imitates his anger. The angry person is adulterous, a friend of the world, an enemy of God (James 4:4). Not surprisingly, the angry person is highly practiced in accusing others and exonerating himself—another signature move of the Devil. All this is why God's words to you have such urgency.

Yet in the midst of this ugliness, God is jealous for you. Anger is a sign that you have turned away from God and followed your own desires and idols. But God doesn't turn away. Instead, he jealously pursues you. Chances are, you have never known someone who wanted you so much that they were jealous when you had divided attention or mixed allegiances. Who else but God loves you so much that he wants you back after such betrayal?

The way back is to confess your sin as against God, thank him for his forgiveness and jealous steadfast love, take time to mourn over the destruction you caused, confess your sin to the ones you fired upon, be astounded if they are inclined to forgive you, ask the Lord for real power to take a stand against your desires, ask everyone you can think of—friends and strangers—to pray for you, wash your mouth out with soap, get savvy as to how the Devil captured your heart, and humble yourself before the Lord. There is lots of good work ahead.

In short, *humble yourself before the Lord, and everything will follow from that.* Up ahead, expect to confess your anger more quickly, and expect to interpret whatever provoked your anger as a test used by God to reveal your heart and draw you back to himself. Expect to grow in patience and gentleness.

ꕥ ꕥ ꕥ

CIRCLE: There is lots to circle here.

REFLECT: What is your version of anger? How does it have the Devil in it?

PRAY: Speak James 4:1–10 as your confession and hope to the Lord.

TALK: The most important conversation is with the person who witnessed your anger.

DAY 29
GENTLENESS

Whoever is slow to anger is better than the mighty,
and he who rules his spirit than he who takes a city.
—*Proverbs 16:32*

Take my yoke upon you, and learn from me, for I am gentle
and lowly in heart, and you will find rest for your souls.
—*Matthew 11:29*

She came out guns loaded. "Why do you always . . ." she said defensively. He couldn't even remember the accusation as he told me the story, but he knew where it was going. Their tradition was set in stone. One would accuse, the other would counter-accuse. Then one would escalate—first louder, then with added flourishes such as nasty name-calling. Then someone would stomp out of the room with as much ruckus as possible. Then, as one of them remembered they were parents and had kids who were witnessing the mass destruction, they would move into cold war mode.

This time was different. He heard his wife's concern, and she was right. He had said he would work on whatever the "always" was, and he hadn't. He had said "yes" to her but did "no" (Matthew 5:37). This is lying, and lying is against God, who only speaks truth. It is also against the person who is betrayed by it. So he responded, "You are right. We have talked about this before, and I said I would not do it again. I can understand that this affects your ability to trust me. Please forgive me. I want to listen and take this seriously."

So simple. When someone is upset with you, you listen to that person. If you've been wrong, you acknowledge it and ask forgiveness. If you don't understand the accusation, ask the person to help you or bring in someone who can help. What could be easier? Yes, this is ordinary, and it is glorious, and it is spiritual. And whenever it happens, it's also a miracle.

There is, of course, a backstory. This husband had awakened to his own anger and pride. Jesus's holy anger and humility had revealed that his selfish anger was always about his own perceived rights and offenses to his pride.

Did you love? For the first time, he asked himself the question, and then everything changed.

Confession *before God* leads to thanks for his free, generous forgiveness, and to rest in what Christ has done. This starts a whole new cycle. When you see your sin and know forgiveness, you are less affected by the accusations of others. You have already confessed more serious matters, and you are ready to listen.

Confession *before the other person* is possible because of God's power working in you. You will notice that as you respond to this power—a.k.a. grace—he loads it on (James 4:6). Confession will feel more natural the next time.

This is the path of those who follow Jesus with a heart that is gentle and lowly (Matthew 11:29). They listen. They are undisturbed and quiet before God (Psalm 131). They are satisfied (Psalm 22:26). They are child-servants. They rest in God's strength and strategize how to bring peace and reconciliation. They are patient and make wise decisions when criticized. They are alert to the weak and oppressed and take a stand to protect them. Their words are so powerful that, in conflicts, they can disarm angry people (Proverbs 15:1). Jesus calls them blessed, and, apparently, these are the ones who will inherit the earth (Matthew 5:5).

ᔓᔕ ᔓᔕ ᔓᔕ

CIRCLE: What is important here? What is hard here?

REFLECT: Think of a conflict you have had. Imagine how spiritual gentleness and humility would have changed it. Powerful men have their power under control.

PRAY: What do you want to ask of your Father?

TALK: Have you seen someone disarm another person through gentleness? Let them know how this encouraged you. (Proverbs 15:1)?

DAY 30
SAY NO

For the grace of God has appeared that offers salvation to all people. It teaches us to say "No" to ungodliness and worldly passions, and to live self-controlled, upright and godly lives in this present age, while we wait for the blessed hope—the appearing of the glory of our great God and Savior, Jesus Christ, who gave himself for us to redeem us from all wickedness and to purify for himself a people that are his very own, eager to do what is good.

—Titus 2:11–14 NIV

Bill once hid his porn habit. His wife would discover his actions, and he would act contrite but go back to it again. Now he doesn't seem to care. His wife remains in the house, but his out-of-control desires have separated him from the person he loves. She was once hurt, then angry, and is now indifferent and building a life apart from him.

Human desires have a lie embedded within them that says, "just a little more." And when you scan the list of sins that are most damaging to a community, Paul identifies anger and its associates—enmity, strife, fits of anger, rivalries, divisions—along with physical desires—sexual immorality, sensuality, drunkenness, orgies (Galatians 5:19–20).

Both anger and physical desires are traps. Anger reveals the paradox of pride. It feels like power. People notice you for a moment, and you might get your way. No wonder it is so popular. It is the perfect drug for powerless people. It is also slavery to your desires. You don't have control. *I want* is your master; sin is your master;

Satan is your master—they are all partners in the dark kingdom, which proclaims that you can be like God rather than under him.

Meanwhile, physical desires whisper that life is short and you are entitled to a little pleasure, and a little turns into a lot. Ephesians says, "They have become callous and have given themselves up to sensuality, greedy to practice every kind of impurity" (4:19).

This all makes sense if Jesus never came and we have no hope. But he did come, and he will come again. He has released his people from the penalty of sin and the power of sin. He will release us from its very presence. You have evidence that you belong to him when you hear his words: "As he who called you is holy, you also be holy in all your conduct" (1 Peter 1:15). When you live under God, you learn to say "no." True power and authority begin by subduing your own desires. Paul writes, "For God gave us a spirit not of fear but of power and love and self-control" (2 Timothy 1:7).

Sanity creeps in when you can say with Paul, "I am unspiritual, sold as a slave to sin. I do not understand what I do. For what I want to do I do not do, but what I hate I do" (Romans 7:14–15 NIV). Then you can work out your own paraphrase of the Titus 2 passage.

> Goodness and lovingkindness and mercy have appeared in Jesus (Titus 3:4–7). That grace wants to rescue me from the slavery of my passions and give me the power to say "no." I have had enough of the lies. I want to be a true human who is controlled by the grace of Christ alone. Self-control is a gift from the Spirit that can actually interrupt that cycle of "yes." Today I imagine that I am saying "no" when I begin to descend into my zombie state and indulge myself. I call on Jesus for help, realizing that this "no" is what Christ has destined me for, and I'm determined to say it before he comes rather than after.

Self-indulgence is easy; just do whatever you want to. Saying "no" when you would prefer to say "yes" is a pinnacle of strength, which you will discover as you pursue humility.

ଓ ଓ ଓ

CIRCLE: Humility is reaching into every area of life. What stands out?

REFLECT: Self-control is among the most important and least discussed issues in this generation. Have you witnessed the disaster of saying yes to desires? It does not go well. Keep working through the Titus 2 passage. Work out your own paraphrase. Then speak your paraphrase out loud.

PRAY: Turn Titus 2 into your words to the Lord.

TALK: Every man needs to have conversations about this.

DAY 31
ASK FOR PRAYER

Pray for me.
—1 Kings 13:6

Brothers, pray for us.
—1 Thessalonians 5:25

Pray for one another.
—James 5:16

Your weakness and neediness are never a burden too heavy for the Lord. And humility means that you can express it to him. In turn, that makes it easier to ask for prayer from others.

We know plenty about prayer. We know that to be known by God and to talk with him is the greatest privilege of life with Christ. We know that he never turns us away but always hears. Many of the Old Testament saints could never understand why God would listen to sinful rascals, and it was the common reason they praised and worshipped him. We also know that our Father is sovereign over all, yet he has decided to include us in the advance of his kingdom, particularly through prayer. Simply put, prayer is the way God gets things done.

We also know that prayer is harder than it seems. I discovered this when a friend and I decided we would pray a half hour each day for a week. If Jesus could pray for an entire night, a half hour didn't seem like too long. Even so, we reconsidered and started with a smaller step, agreeing on ten minutes a day. And we both fell short. Praying is hard work. Asking other people to pray for you is harder.

Today, lean into asking for prayer. What do you need most deeply? It is good for you to ask for prayer about these things, and it's good for those who pray for you. Try not to major in the common requests for health and healing.[11] If that's all you ever share, you are afraid and still thinking about your reputation.

Jesus identifies Peter's deepest need for prayer when he says, "I have prayed for you that your faith may not fail" (Luke 22:32; see also Hebrews 12:3–4). Where is your faith most prone to fail? When do you feel especially weak? What situations? What sins seem to look like life even though you know they bring death? What mistreatment from your past has shut you down and left you spiritually vulnerable? Have you spoken openly about same-sex attraction or other sexual struggles that leave you feeling isolated? Do you really believe that you have been forgiven in Jesus's death? Answering these questions will get to some of your deepest needs.

Have you ever been in a small group when it was time to pray and people bring their requests: sick aunts, job interviews, a visit to family that might be difficult. Then someone asks for prayer for a future business trip when he has too much time and a TV with porn just a click away. He wants to be strengthened to fight. He mentions some things that have helped in the past, and he plans to take those actions again. Someone volunteers to call him in the evenings while he is gone. The group prays. And the remaining requests are different: a hard marriage, a parent whose relationship with an adult child has fallen apart, a young man who is beginning to address abuse in his past and wants to face it by faith. All it takes is one person who is willing to say that he struggles with sin for the community to come together. Humility is a natural leader. Yes, you risk hearing words of condemnation from someone who looks down on you, but the combination of desperation and humility is not silenced by a few discouraging words.

If you are still not ready for that step, you could begin with the smaller step of confessing that your love falls far short of the love of Christ for a spouse, child, or neighbor. Before you ask for prayer, find a Scripture passage that can guide you and the other person in how to pray and review how you have tried to fight the spiritual battle so far.

Be careful of good intentions. For example, you intend to ask a friend at church for prayer, but you get sidetracked by someone else. A better way is to text your friend after you have thought about how you want him to pray. Arrange for a brief time to meet, and ask the person to pray for you then and there.

Neediness before others is not easy. But it is excellent for your soul, and it is a fine way to lead.

ᔓ ᔓ ᔓ

CIRCLE: What is most important for you?

REFLECT: For the next week, pray for your heart more than your circumstances or discomfort. Just your heart. There you need more of Christ, and more power to do what he commands.

PRAY: Speak to the Lord about those needs.

TALK: Ask someone to pray for one of the struggles of your heart.

DAY 32
WAKE UP

These men who have turned the world upside down have come here also, and Jason has received them, and they are all acting against the decrees of Caesar, saying that there is another king, Jesus.
—Acts 17:6–7

A purpose statement with such dramatic changes is hard to pass up, especially when meaning and purpose are disappearing from daily life. And turning the world upside down is still the mission of all who follow King Jesus. How does it happen? Jesus is with you, and you put the power of God on display each day, in small steps. His kingdom will cover the earth at his glorious appearing, and you are part of that mission.

Humility, one specific and neglected expression of this power, is coming into focus. You see how pride takes you captive and always damages the people around you. You have confessed your sin to someone and been forgiven. You are thankful that the Spirit of God has given you strength to ask for forgiveness and that God's power can even heal relationships.

Now keep that momentum going. Confession of sin is the beginning. *Then* the battle with sin has begun. It has been called *repentance*. If you really want to do serious battle and cut the head off the snake rather than scare it off, it is called *mortification*, which means that you are going to keep fighting until you put that sin to death (Colossians 3:5). Now is the time to dabble in mortification. As you do, remember that grace brings even more grace from God.

The more you fight, the more grace you receive. This is why you don't simply ask for prayer that you would stop drinking so much. Prayer coexists with a plan of attack.

Consider a common occurrence for a married man. Your wife has asked you for the umpteenth time for something specific—to call if you will be late, clean up your dishes, engage with the children, get off your screen and talk. Perhaps your conscience is finally affected by those small inadvertent omissions. Now what?

- Confess your sin to your wife, on your knees, at least metaphorically. If you are going to contribute to the world being turned upside down, *you will be more concerned about your sin than she is.*
- If she responds with anger and raises other ways you have hurt her, you are all ears. You have no résumé to defend. If her comments are on the mark, that gives you more to confess. If you don't understand, ask for help. Notice the strength and resiliency of humility in all this.
- Identify how your sin is against God, which begins the process of mortification. "Against you, you only, have I sinned" (Psalm 51:4). If you are not listening to your spouse and are instead taking her words casually, you are not listening to the Lord either. If you say you will do something and don't, you imitate Satan's lies. If you are unfaithful in small things, how can she trust you in anything? To paraphrase the apostle Paul, *When you pursue sin, you pursue death* (Romans 7:5). You are hostile to God. Pray through this and ask the Lord to teach you to "mourn and weep" (James 4:9).
- Consider what is the opposite of your sin. Take off your pride and put on . . . ?
- Know yourself. You sin against your wife because you want what you want. Your sin is not a mistake. What is going on in your heart? What interferes with you letting your yes be yes? Do you "forget"? Then how will you remember? Tattoo it

on your face? Set an alarm? Take action right away. "I forgot" might be truthful, but it also says that there is something more important to you than the other person's words.
- Check your plan out with a friend. Ask other men to pray for you. Consider where and how your plan might break down.

Most of us have never created an action plan like this. *When your sin has impacted a relationship, you should be more concerned about your sin than the person you offended is concerned.* Your confession includes a ruthless plan of attack. Jesus commends this approach to you, "If your right eye causes you to sin, tear it out and throw it away" (Matthew 5:29). Leave no wiggle room. This is the way of humility that listens to God and others. So make a plan with the help of other people—a plan with actual, workable, measurable ideas. For instance, if online dangers are your battle, purchase an app that will share all the sites you visit with two other men, even if the person betrayed says it is unnecessary and you are already reviewing the five ways you might try to circumvent that plan.

Will this inconvenience you? You hope so. No one said it would be easy to turn the world upside down. This is a powerful place to start. Ahead, you can learn to get mad at your sin. "To fear the Lord is to hate evil; I hate pride and arrogance" (Proverbs 8:13 NIV). All this is possible because you know the Spirit himself convicts us of sin and the Son assures us that we are forgiven and pleasing.

ေ ေ ေ

CIRCLE: This one is not easy. Circle one thing that seems important.

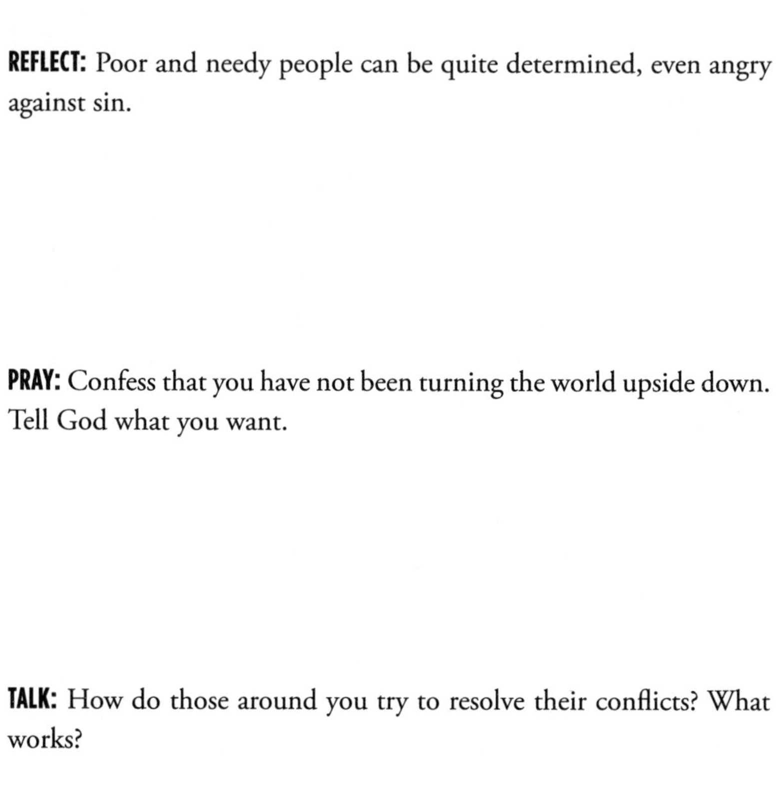

REFLECT: Poor and needy people can be quite determined, even angry against sin.

PRAY: Confess that you have not been turning the world upside down. Tell God what you want.

TALK: How do those around you try to resolve their conflicts? What works?

DAY 33
SHAME

Behold, I stand at the door and knock. If anyone hears my voice and opens the door, I will come in to him and eat with him, and he with me.
—*Revelation 3:20*

John Lennon was the most contentious member of the Beatles. He seemed arrogant and prideful, and he was. But there was more. Some of the harder edges wore away around the same time he wrote a song he entitled, "Mother," which included the line that he wanted his mother, but she didn't want him. That was his bravest song. Men usually prefer to do anything except reveal shameful rejection and how that rejection still hurts.

Shame is the most painful of human experiences. It means that you are unacceptable and different from those in the community around you—or you would be if they really knew you. Feeling worthless and unlovable become daily companions. Shame has three different causes:

1. It could be from sins that leave people shocked. Sins such as child abuse, domestic violence, embezzlement, or fraudulent ways to get money that oppress the poor or elderly. These are among those secret sins that it is best to reveal so that they will lose their power over you.
2. It could be from public failures that are not sins, but still cause shame, such as being fired from a job, divorced, or in a car accident that seriously injured other people.

3. It could be from people who have treated you disgracefully, who were supposed to love you but did not, who violated you, or who humiliated you with words or deeds. This shame can be the most life dominating.

In response, you search for an acceptable identity, you numb through various addictions, or you determine not to get close again. Whatever your strategy, relationships cannot flourish when you have such a secret. This is why Jesus went to extremes for you.

Read through any gospel account and you will notice that Jesus is an outcast who spends his time with outcasts. He pursues them, eats with them, heals them, and makes them clean. Shame is about who you are connected to. You were identified by the people who heaped shame on you, but now you are connected to Jesus Christ, by faith, and you receive the honor of being a friend of God. Notice this connection in how he pursues outcasts and literally touches them. In that touch, he gives you his holiness and cleansing, and he takes your shame on himself (see Luke 8:43–48), only to take shame and sin to the cross and obliterate them. When reading the New Testament, you would think that the kingdom of God is only for those who have been forsaken, abused, or discarded.

Shame can give humility a bad name, but the difference between humiliation and humility is great. Humiliation is to be alone, disgraced, and laid low by another. Humility is to walk with (listen to) the Servant-King for the good of others. In this dependent relationship, we learn about his steadfast love, we have no reason to hide, and the wickedness of others no longer defines us.

The good news Jesus proclaimed runs deep for those familiar with shame. For now, forsake the lie that you are excluded from Christ's body. Humble yourself before the Lord, which means that you listen to him more than the voices from your past. As one outcast to another, he recognizes you, knocks on your door, and wants to eat a meal with you. In that meal he says that you are his and he is yours. Speak to him about this while you share that meal.

Once you have become more comfortable in a conversation with Jesus about your shame, then it is time to speak to those who are closest to you. What you hide gives power to the thing hidden and distances you from other people. In God's family, we speak with each other about what is good and what is painful.

ഗ ഗ ഗ

CIRCLE: What in this gets you thinking?

REFLECT: Shame is so resistant to coming into the open. But please know that unattended shame only gathers more strength. Humility asks for help.[12] Where do you see shame in your life? Where do you hide? What lies about you and Jesus are attached to your shame?

PRAY: Talk to the Lord. Tell him what you know of his true response to you.

TALK: Almost every man is familiar with shame, though it can be buried deep. Could you imagine talking to another man about this?

DAY 34
COMPASSION

His father saw him and felt compassion.
—Luke 15:20

The wayward son left dishonorably, with money from the father and no thought of returning. Yet, after the son spent years away, when the father heard that his destitute and ungrateful son might be on his way home, he was so moved with compassion that he ran to greet his unfaithful son and throw him a party. The father's welcome home did not include "I told you so," or any words of advice. Jesus told this story about unfaithful people who return to the Father. Before they have even come close, the Father runs to them, and he invents ways to show them favor.

You receive the compassion of the Father. If the disgraced son receives the father's compassion, you certainly have aroused his compassion. He knows your troubles, and he wants to hear them from you.

The story of the prodigal son links to humility because receiving God's compassion requires you to listen to him and believe what he says. You, in turn, give the compassion of Christ as you hold onto the concerns of others and are moved by them. First, you must confront some questions that are more about you:

Does his compassion matter to you?
Do you receive it?
Do you insist that you are an unlovable exception to his grace?
Do you avoid him because you hold him responsible for your struggles?

Humility listens. Meanwhile, the Devil lies about God ("his love doesn't quite reach you") and about you ("you are on your own"). If these lies interfere with your listening, humility simply gets help, bringing the lies into the open so that other people can stand with you. If you want more help, hear the question that Jesus asked Peter: "Do you love me?" In other words, "You know I love you. Do you love me?" This is a kind of unselfing that helps you hear and believe.

You offer the compassion of Christ. Meanwhile, humility makes you more aware of the hardships around you as you consider the interests of others. Take a moment to see those hardships, of other men, your spouse, your children—those who are going through something painful. You can be sure that trouble follows all of us each day. Then do something. Humility takes initiative.

Be thoughtful about how "doing something" can reflect God's compassion. Avoid starting any conversation with words like these:

- It could have been worse . . .
- When this happened to me . . .
- Have you tried . . . ?

Consider what words have been unhelpful to you and what words build you up. Usually, advice is unhelpful, especially unsolicited advice. Advice comes from teachers, experts, and consultants—people *above* the suffering person who have a simple answer for hard things. Advice doesn't pray. It doesn't consider love. Even when advice is good, it is wrong. Advice is more interested in being right than in compassion. Better to confess you need it than offer it.

Humility listens and is moved by what is on the other's heart. It is present, listens, and cares. Humility brings people together. Humility says things like:

- Are you okay?
- Anything hard this week?
- Ugh. I'm so sorry. Is there any way I can help?

- Please, can you say more about that? It seems like it was pretty painful.
- How should I pray for you? Let's pray right now.
- I want you to know that you have been on my heart. You aren't alone.

And humility remembers: "Here is one way I have prayed for you."

Most men are slow to show compassion. God never is (see Psalm 10, 13, or any psalm of lament).

☙ ☙ ☙

CIRCLE: There is a lot here. What is important for you?

REFLECT: Where does receiving and offering God's compassion break down for you? Why?

PRAY: Speak to the Lord about how you receive and give his compassion.

TALK: Who will you approach with compassion?

DAY 35
INSULTS AND OFFENSES

If your brother sins against you, go and tell him his fault, between you and him alone. If he listens to you, you have gained your brother. But if he does not listen, take one or two others along with you.
—Matthew 18:15–16

"I don't like you," a five-year-old said to a colleague of mine at a Christmas party. The boy had never met the man, who responded, "I am so sorry. Is there any reason why?" But the young boy was already gone. We chuckled about it and continued our conversation. Some offenses are easy to overlook.

The proud have the hardest time overlooking insults. They are the most insecure and defensive. Every offense or perceived offense is a lethal blow. That is how life is when you must fend for yourself—no one else will protect you. But a servant of the King, who confesses sins daily, who knows that his Father is the righteous Judge, who knows that all good things have come to him as a gift, and who remembers that he is unworthy of the favor God has shown him, is not easily provoked or offended.

Consider Jesus's words about those who slap you across the face with a biting insult or a string of curses: "Do not resist the one who is evil. But if anyone slaps you on the right cheek, turn to him the other also" (Matthew 5:39). Gentleness is about strength with restraint; reactive anger that curses back is weakness. If you have earned the insult, you can apologize with sincerity. Otherwise, you leave the person to your Father, who is the righteous Judge, and then you are given an opportunity to treat others as you have been treated by

God. Since you have not been treated as your sins deserve, perhaps you can respond as my colleague did to the young boy.

But what if the insult came from a person in your church or a family member? A father and husband committed himself to being a servant, which meant to him that he would quietly serve his family without complaint, oblivious to reckless or hurtful words. After two days, his mission left him despondent and isolated. We overlook offenses from an anonymous person in a shopping line. When words from those closer to us sting, we speak openly, which is much harder than silence. Remember that humility's strategic goal is to build people up and bring them together. When reckless words separate, we consider how to mend the tear. You could say, "Ouch, that was pretty harsh." But humility might be tested when the other person responds, "Why are you so overly sensitive?" Or, "I didn't mean anything by it." So you persist wisely—"Could we talk about it?"—and do what you can to close the gap between you.

Sometimes you overlook offenses. Other times you speak about offenses for the good of the relationship and the good of the offending person. Silence with grumbling is easy. Avoidance with resentment is easy, but covering offenses has its challenges. Speaking to the person who sinned is spiritual—you need power that is not your own.

Humility is not flammable and quick to react, but it certainly is not committed to silence. It moves into difficult relationships with a desire to listen, courage to speak openly, and a heart that is poor and needy for the Spirit's power.

 csɔ csɔ csɔ

CIRCLE: This is real strength. What do you hear?

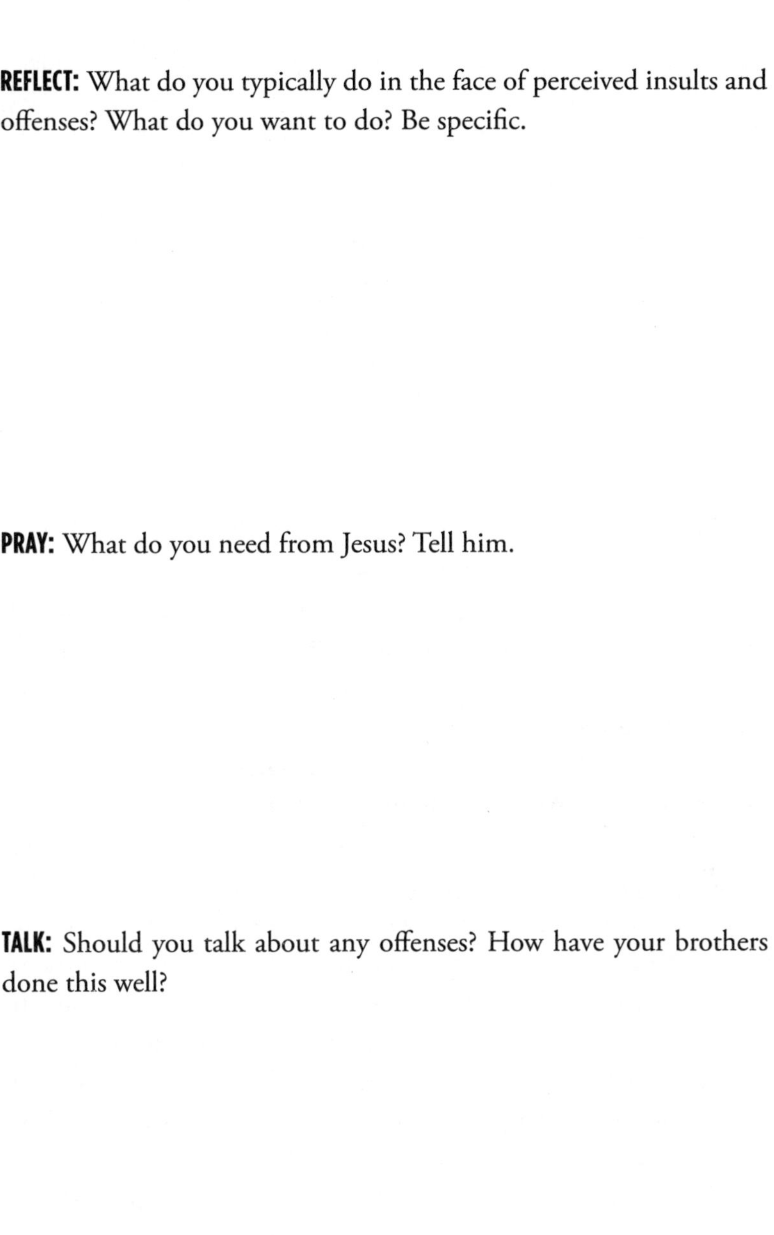

REFLECT: What do you typically do in the face of perceived insults and offenses? What do you want to do? Be specific.

PRAY: What do you need from Jesus? Tell him.

TALK: Should you talk about any offenses? How have your brothers done this well?

DAY 36
SEE GOOD

Outdo one another in showing honor.
—*Romans 12:10*

The apostle Paul usually begins his letters with gratitude. "I give thanks to my God always for you because of the grace of God that was given you in Christ Jesus" (1 Corinthians 1:4). Then he boasts about the recipients and writes that he always prays for them. He has seen the goodness of God in them, and when you see Christ in other people you just have to say something.

Since Jesus Christ is King, and the Spirit of Jesus has come, we expect to see evidence of him everywhere. His goodness can be witnessed even in those who don't know him. Right now, think of two people in whom you see something of God's goodness. A generous neighbor, a preacher whose words were helpful, a colleague who had a great idea, a family member who is patient, or a friend you have seen grow in Christ. If you are married, add your spouse to this list and identify five ways she reflects the goodness of God to you and others. If you have a cantankerous child, include them. In fact, identify one good thing in all your children. Then say something to these people.

Now increase the difficulty. Who is your perceived competition? They might be better than you at something you find important. Where do you see good in them? Who has received the job they wanted? Who is happy because of some pleasant circumstance in his life? These circumstances don't usually last too long, so if you know someone who is celebrating something good, join the celebration and be happy for him. "Rejoice with those who rejoice" (Romans 12:15). You can usually muster up some celebration for a person's birthday, but humility gives you the power to honor him during the offseason. The goodness of God is all around you. Your job is to savor it and draw attention to it.

How can this be genuine appreciation? If you truly love a person, it is easy. Men are not known for the skill of seeing good things in others. Usually we can do it for those we love such as family or children—whom we don't feel competitive toward. But comparisons still run deep in our souls, as does discontent and the desire for more. C. S. Lewis wrote, "Pride gets no pleasure out of having something, only out of having more of it than the next man."[13] When pride gets in our way, our praise of others can diminish, as though there is only so much praise to go around. So, once again, you discover that everything is spiritual on this path of humility—it is not natural to us, and we need the Spirit's power.

See good in those who immediately come to mind. Don't settle for saying, "Thanks for your good words." Instead, make sure you have their attention, and then speak about how you have been built up by what you have seen in them. Here are some ideas to jumpstart your thinking:

- To a child: "I have to tell you something. I was thinking about what you did when your brother wanted something you were using. You could have just told him that he couldn't have it, but instead you let him use it. You are an amazing peacemaker. You are patient and kind, and I want to be like that."
- To a friend: "I have had two conversations in the last week with people who mentioned your care for them—your hospitality, your notes of encouragement, your genuine interest in them. You are a pastor who cares so well for a lot of people. It all reminded me that I have also been encouraged by your care for my own soul. Thank you, brother."

The Spirit works through Scripture and through other people. Don't miss an opportunity. Take time to send out a text that honors another man. Speak words that draw attention to the people God uses to encourage you.

ꕥ ꕥ ꕥ

CIRCLE: Circle "See good." Any other highlights?

REFLECT: Do you see the good in others? Do you speak about it?

PRAY: Think of one person. Ask Jesus to give you good words that you can speak to that person.

TALK: Speak it soon. Talk to one person you live with and one person you don't. Write, call, say something.

DAY 37

QUICK TO LISTEN

Everyone should be quick to listen,
slow to speak and slow to become angry.
—*James 1:19 NIV*

Humility has a purpose. As we turn the world upside down, it begins with Christ's church, "building up the body of Christ, until we all attain to the unity of the faith and of the knowledge of the Son of God" (Ephesians 4:12–13). The goal is to draw a diverse people together in Christ. One way to do this is to look for what is good in others. When you see it, you say something, which is a type of blessing. A blessing includes both the good words you speak and your prayer that God will make those good things thrive. That is the enjoyable part of pursuing unity. The hard part is that, when people gather, there are always conflicts. So we turn again to listening.

Conflicts are the worst. If you are not experiencing one now, you can still feel the sting of the last one. But we are men who are learning how life works in the kingdom of the risen Jesus, and, in our new world, conflicts are opportunities. They are inevitable. They also leave you no choice but to say to the Lord, "Help!" *That* is an opportunity. Then, as we go through them with spiritual wisdom, conflicts allow the world around us to see the Spirit on display. They can be painful opportunities, but opportunities all the same.

The Spirit begins his good work as we pay attention to our own hearts (Luke 17:3). This follows Jesus's words to "first take the log out of your own eye" (Matthew 7:5). That log includes believing that we are right. Trace our differences in politics, theology, parenting, or anything else and you find, "I know the truth." "If you knew what I know, you would agree with me. If you don't agree, then you're biased by a delusional ideology or self-interest, of which I am free."[14] Humility begins when you realize that you don't actually know all truth, and that God has determined that we learn from him and each other.

If you have already been quick to speak and slow to listen, then you have opportunities to ask forgiveness. *That* turns the world upside down. Don't be distracted by excuses such as, "she (or he) was even worse." That is just another version of prideful comparisons. Go and ask forgiveness as soon as possible. Own your sin, sincerely, without expectations that people will say the same thing back to you. Then you are ready to listen. If you hear something that you don't understand, ask for clarification. Listen in a way so that you can communicate to people *why* they believe what they believe. This, of course, is so difficult.

Now listen to a family member or friend who drives you crazy. Imagine this: "I'm sure you have good reasons for what you believe. Please help me to understand them." Consider a child who didn't turn in his homework again: "Son, homework can be miserable. Who would want to do it? But let's think about this together. I wonder what makes it hard for *you*. Tell me the story of when you don't get your homework done. How does that happen? Let's try to figure it out together."

In conflicts, you aim to listen more than talk. As you do, you will find a rule that works in most relationships: The better you understand someone, the more patient you will be and the more you will like the person. It begins with humility that listens.

ᔓ ᔓ ᔓ

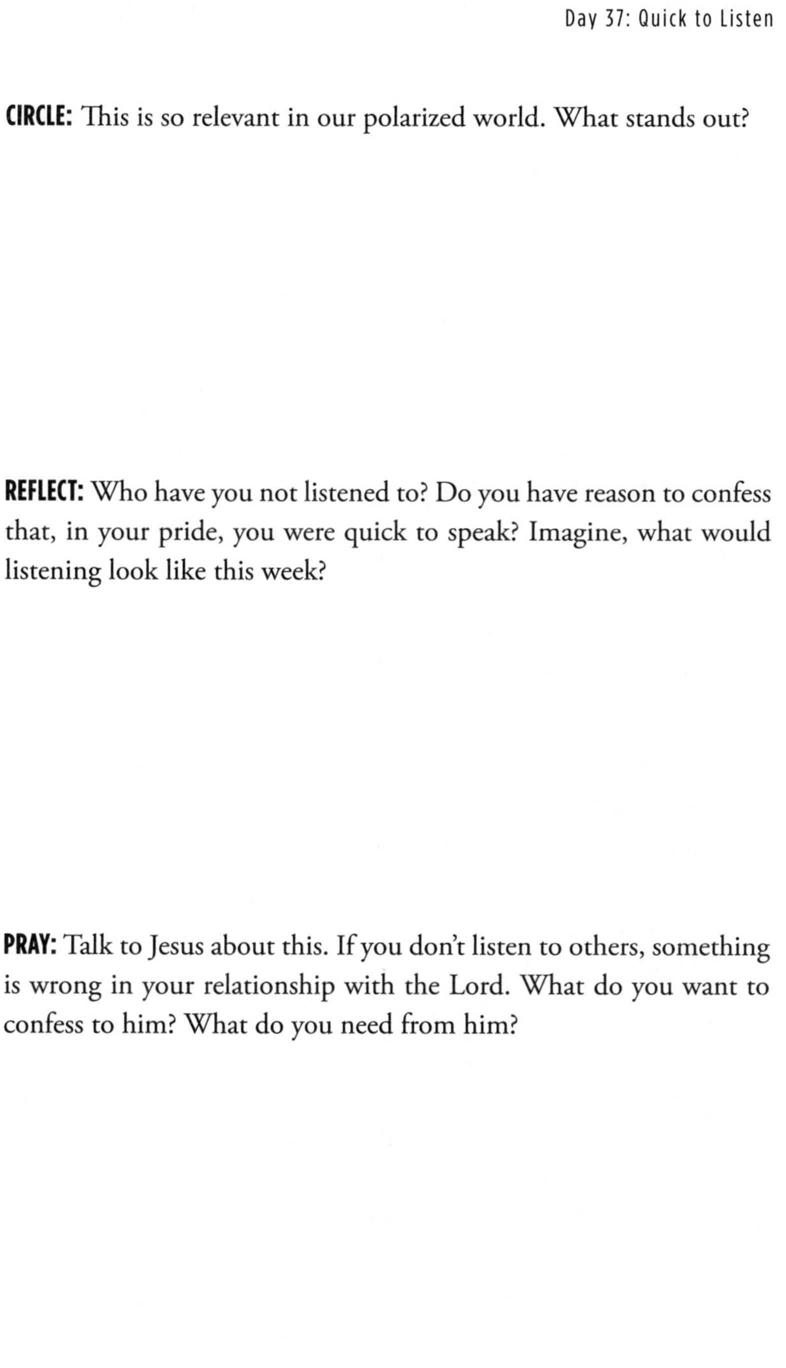

CIRCLE: This is so relevant in our polarized world. What stands out?

REFLECT: Who have you not listened to? Do you have reason to confess that, in your pride, you were quick to speak? Imagine, what would listening look like this week?

PRAY: Talk to Jesus about this. If you don't listen to others, something is wrong in your relationship with the Lord. What do you want to confess to him? What do you need from him?

TALK: Confess to someone you have wronged.

DAY 38
BE INTERESTED

So if there is any encouragement in Christ . . . Do nothing from selfish ambition or conceit, but in humility count others more significant than yourselves. Let each of you look not only to his own interests, but also to the interests of others.
—Philippians 2:1, 3–4

Humility has an interest in others. It is curious and wants to know people deeply. Humility results in you asking questions.

- What has been most important from the last week? What were the best things, the hardest things, the most frightening things, the most surprising things?
- What's been on your heart?
- How are *you*?
- How can I help?

In the passage today, Paul gives three illustrations of those who care about the interests of others. Paul's first illustration is Jesus himself—God himself who became your servant, even to death (Philippians 2:8). Then he writes about Timothy: "I have no one like him, who will be genuinely concerned for your welfare" (v. 20). And then he writes of Epaphroditus (vv. 25–30). Paul is always looking for the good in others that he can honor. Epaphroditus cared about others to the point where, even when ill and close to death, he was more concerned about how the church would be distressed than he was about his own plight.

Now join them. Elevate the interests of others and place them on your heart. It begins with knowing a person's interests. So you listen when people talk. What do they get excited about? I spoke to a man who was looking forward to a fishing trip. Even though fishing is not exciting to me, it was to him. So I asked, "Where are you going? What do you especially enjoy about fishing?" Those questions were all I needed to know his deeper interests. He responded, "I will be going with my son, and I haven't seen him in a year." *That* is exciting, and I couldn't wait to hear all about it. No matter how much you like fishing, love for another person is deeper and more important.

What troubles them? A neighbor is getting a cancerous lesion removed. All he knows is that it is some kind of cancer, it is on his face, and the surgeon doesn't know what he will find. You make a note to remember the date of the surgery so that you can send a text before: "Hey, I am hoping it goes well." You can follow up with a brief visit when he gets home. These are small things, but most people have never experienced that level of concern or interest.

If a conversation seems stuck in small talk about weather and sports, keep listening for pleasures and troubles. Don't give up until you enjoy or admire that person just a little more. Here are some possible conversation movers:

- Seems like it was a hard week.
- I think your interest in football is more than just football. It is about friends, an opportunity to get together, celebrate together, complain together. It is about participating in a community. You seem to be good at that.
- Do you enjoy your work? What is it that you enjoy about it?
- That's really interesting. Tell me more about it.

Life, of course, is more than pleasures and troubles. Scripture identifies the heart as deep (Proverbs 20:5). If you want to go deeper with someone, aim to talk about eternal matters: our knowledge of God and our rest in him, the hinderances to following him, and the temptations that lie about what is good.

I was talking on the phone to an old friend I hadn't spoken to in a year when he recounted the mounting hardships in his family. I cared, and he knew it, but our conversations could leave affection and concern assumed rather than said. This time I could think of no elegant transition to spiritual things, so I just blurted out, "This stuff is overwhelming. I am going to pray for you right now." In an email a few days later, he expressed his appreciation and asked how he could pray for me and my family—something that had never happened before.

Humility and love are creative. If you are interested in knowing what is on a person's heart, you will find a way to uncover it.

ଓ ଓ ଓ

CIRCLE: This devotion identifies humility's interest in others. What phrases caught your attention?

REFLECT: We want to know others because God knows us. Who does that well for you? What is on the heart of two people around you? One goal could be to know a person well enough to pray for them.

PRAY: Talk to the Lord about people you enjoy and people who need prayer.

TALK: What is your plan for knowing one person a little better today?

DAY 39

WISE WORDS

There is one whose rash words are like sword thrusts,
but the tongue of the wise brings healing.
—Proverbs 12:18

A word fitly spoken is like apples of gold in a setting of silver. Like a gold ring or an ornament of gold is a wise reprover to a listening ear.
—Proverbs 25:11–12

Humility before God always pushes you past mere knowledge and into actual words you speak to him. Humility before other people pushes you past good intentions and is most often expressed in words. God's house is a talkative one.

You know that your tongue can set destructive fires and pierce like a sword. You know it can tear down and break relationships. A father was doing some spackling and painting when his ten-year-old son came to help, or simply to be closer to his dad. When the son accidently kicked over a small can of paint the father exploded, "Why do you make everything harder?" In a moment, the father saw that his son was undone and he quickly apologized, but it was too late. It was as though he had branded his son with words that would stay with him for years to come. The father finally understood that his tongue could kill, and it was the occasion for him to submit himself and his words to Jesus Christ.

With this awareness in mind, we set out to submit our words to Jesus, scrutinizing them, refining them. We want our speech crammed with words of life. Take time to review some good words that you have spoken or heard from other wise people. Here are some examples:

- Text someone who is on your heart. You could text how you prayed for that person.
- Ask a spouse or children:
    - What was surprising about your day?
    - Tell me more about someone who is a good friend. What do you appreciate about that person?
    - What is troubling to you today?
    - Could you pray for me this morning? I am anxious about . . .
- Ask a friend, "What was the best thing from your week? What was the worst thing?"
- If you were helped by a sermon, text the preacher and mention one specific point that was helpful.
- Ask someone about his children. Share his interest in his children. You can start with knowing the kids' names. Know enough to be able to pray for one of them.
- If you know about a person's hobbies, ask what it is that they especially enjoy about them.
- Live as though you just happen to be talking to someone on their birthday.
- Tell someone how they have helped you and that you are thankful.

Perhaps you pray something like this and enter into an agreement with like-minded men:

> Lord, I confess that my words to you are too few. If I knew that I was poor, needy, and thankful, I would have much more to say. I want to hear your words and speak more words back to you. When I speak with others, I want to use words that are "like apples of gold in a setting of silver" (Proverbs 25:11). I want words that invite those who are reluctant to be more open, words that ask for

help, words that build people up and bring them together, words that are willing to ask hard questions and ask about temptations, words that bless. These words come as you teach me that all your words are good.

ꕥ ꕥ ꕥ

CIRCLE: This should sound familiar. The way we use our words is such an important part of life with Christ. What stands out?

REFLECT: Is this hard or easy for you? When have your words been reckless this week? What would have been more suitable words? How do you hope to speak good words to someone today?

PRAY: Pray your version of the prayer above.

TALK: Today, be alert to your conversations. Take a small step by speaking good words to someone. It could be as simple as "thank you," with specific ways you have appreciated what the person has said or done.

DAY 40
CONFIDENCE, BOASTING, AND REST

Humble yourselves, therefore, under the mighty hand of God so that at the proper time he may exalt you, casting all your anxieties on him, because he cares for you.
—1 Peter 5:6–7

You can be sure that every man lives with more fear and anxiety than he is willing to say. It just so happens that *confidence* is humility's unexpected partner. In fact, confidence cannot exist apart from humility. Your confidence is only as steady as what you trust in. If you trust in yourself, your ego was never intended to carry that freight and all you can do is try to prop it up. If you trust in other people or money, they can give you some temporary strength, but money can't rescue you from shame and death.

You were designed to rest in—to need—God alone. "My soul finds rest in God alone; my salvation comes from him. He alone is my rock and my salvation; he is my fortress, I will never be shaken" (Psalm 62:1–2 NIV 1984).

I remember waking up one day and thinking, *Everything is just right.* The children were healthy, my wife was lying next to me, our relationship was warm and without conflict, I had work I enjoyed, and the sky was clear with hints of red as I looked out the window. For some unknown reason, the realities of the day waited a good ten seconds before they came at me one after another, messengers of anxiety, until I popped out of bed, wondering where to start and knowing that there were far too many items I could do nothing about. If only we had an alternative to those relentless anxieties.

And we do have an alternative. Humbling ourselves is the remedy. Listen to the Lord, trust what he says, believe that he cares. Peter's words in today's passage can be paraphrased like this:

> Your Father cares for you at all times. Jesus has secured forgiveness of your sins, and those sins were the only thing that could separate you. Now nothing can separate you from God. Do you believe that the Father cares, even in those details that are so painful? Do you really? Your Father has sworn himself to you. Your job is to walk humbly with him. One way to do that is to speak to him of the troubles and anxieties of the day. Don't keep them to yourself. He will take those matters and "worry" about them on your behalf. You can then live as his child who trusts him and consider how to honor him through your simple obedience today.

As you engage with the Lord by speaking, responding, and believing, you will notice that your anxieties become mixed with confidence that God is with you and that he does care. If you want to get even more serious about confidence, you could indulge in some boasting.

> "Let him who boasts boast in this, that he understands and knows me, that I am the LORD who practices steadfast love, justice, and righteousness in the earth. For in these things I delight, declares the LORD." (Jeremiah 9:24)

Humility and confidence are about being connected to the right person. Only then are you unshakable.

ᔓ ᔓ ᔓ

CIRCLE: What stands out?

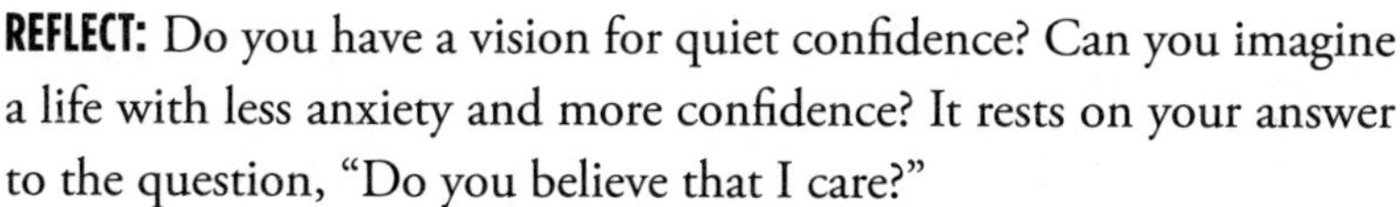

REFLECT: Do you have a vision for quiet confidence? Can you imagine a life with less anxiety and more confidence? It rests on your answer to the question, "Do you believe that I care?"

PRAY: Speak to the Lord about his care. What is "casting all your anxieties on him"? It is, at least, speaking them to him.

TALK: Everyone has fears; humility is a surprising way to be less burdened by them. If you are married, your spouse would be honored to hear of your fears and pray for your confidence, which tends to look like courage.

DAY 41

YOU FIRST

Go therefore and make disciples of all nations.
—*Matthew 28:19*

Overcome evil with good.
—*Romans 12:21*

As humility gathers momentum, so does the spiritual battle. Pride is a nasty enemy. Denying yourself and taking up your cross is not for the weak. Among your identities is *warrior*, who battles first with your own tendencies toward sin and the Devil's partnership in it.

The battle will usually feel like a keen sense of purpose. You listen to the Lord and find there is a job to be done, and you don't need to impress or be controlled by opinions. Failure is no longer an issue because God assured us that his kingdom will extend its borders. You approach life—people, work, and rest—with a clear mission and confidence that you have been brought into God's plans. Then everything has more meaning and purpose. Boredom is impossible. Humility means that you submit to God and his words. You listen and live by them, and then you go out, serving God prayerfully and creatively, seeking advice, and taking small steps that fit your strengths and weaknesses.

You go first in relationships. Humility results in the desire to love others and put them first. In your dealings with people, you love first, confess first, ask for prayer first, send a text first, pray first. You listen with purpose and intent. You ask questions when you don't understand. You remember what is important to people. You invent ways to bless, with a letter, email, or text, with words that are thoughtful. If you pursue others more than they pursue you, so be it. Rejection still hurts, but it doesn't control you.

Your ears are open wide to the suffering of others. You are limited, and suffering is everywhere, so you will often respond with, "Father, your kingdom come." But when that suffering is local, within your family, neighborhood, or church, you speak words of compassion.

You also hear injustices. When someone speaks about past injustices, you slow the conversation and ask how those past injustices have been carried to the present. You also know that there are injustices all around you. Spouses are abused, children are sinned against, and the strong take advantage of the weak. The shame around such things keeps them secret, but you draw out the deep waters of the heart.

You go first at work. You are more active in work too. You work "as you would [for] Christ, not by the way of eye-service, as people-pleasers, but as bondservants of Christ, doing the will of God from the heart" (Ephesians 6:5–6). You do what you say you will do. You speak well of coworkers and make the case for their good work not to be overlooked. You see the good in others, and you enjoy them. When you read Paul's words about work, you notice there is a call to pursue the will of God from your heart. Whatever specifics that includes for you, it will keep you busy for years to come.

You go first in worship. You talk about the sermon, and you tell the preacher one thing that was especially important for you. You actually sing when worship includes singing. You pray at prayer meetings.

You go first in rest. Perhaps the most significant initiatives will come as you ponder the connection between humility and rest. Rest is only possible when you live under the God who is awake and busy, and you rest in him as his child. Human rest includes sleep and care for our bodies, yet this is never isolated from spiritual practices. It is gradually being detached from entertainment, digital diversions and "me time" (which is less restorative than you give it credit for). Humility understands those things that are most important.

All this is not to add new stresses to your life. The feel of humility is rest, contentment, and clarity on what is important, with a deeper sense of meaning and calling.

ෆ ෆ ෆ

CIRCLE: What stands out?

REFLECT: Notice the movement of humility. Simple submission to the Lord and neediness before him leads to a life that is fuller and richer, not just busier. It should feel like you are becoming more like your true self. Where does the freedom of humility open new initiatives for you?

PRAY: Talk to the Lord about where your mind begins to apply this new boldness.

TALK: This is worth asking someone to pray for you.

DAY 42
YOUR STORY

I received mercy.
—1 Timothy 1:16

If you are to walk around comfortable in your own skin, not always having to burnish an image, it helps to have pieced together your story. If you feel like a nobody, he puts you first (Matthew 20:16). God chose you and loved you before he even created the earth (Ephesians 1:4). He says your less-seen contributions to his kingdom are the most critical (1 Corinthians 12:23). You are a bright light to the world (Matthew 5:16), promised to be fruitful as you abide in Jesus (John 15:7-8). You are royalty and heirs of the earth itself (Revelation 21). Yet Paul says you can burn your accomplishments (Philippians 3:4–7). Good works? Don't advertise them, even to yourself. You are a child of God, brother of Jesus, and yet you are nothing special in yourself. God invites the nobodies of the world (1 Corinthians 1:26–29). In other words, this is a complicated story to tell.

Notice how the Lord teaches Israel their corporate story, knowing that they are prone to leaving him out of that story:

> The Lord your God has chosen you to be a people for his treasured possession, out of all the peoples who are on the face of the earth. It was not because you were more in number than any other people that the Lord set his love on you and chose you, for you were the fewest of all peoples, but it is because the Lord loves you. (Deuteronomy 7:6–8)

A second story is given by the apostle Paul. He told his story in all sorts of ways. Once, he described himself as the chief of sinners who received great mercy (1 Timothy 1:15–16). The short version of his story is better known: "For to me to live is Christ, and to die is gain" (Philippians 1:21). Shorter still, "I received mercy."

Your story, too, can be told in many different ways. It could be the story of work you enjoy. It could be a story of relationships. This story is about pride and humility. Or, to adopt both Israel's story and Paul's, this story is about God.

What people shaped your story? How did people lead you toward Christ and wisdom? How did they lead you toward independence and self-effort? Parents, teachers, relatives, neighbors, coaches, or friends. Some bless and build up. They see good things in you that you didn't see. Others tear down. You were never quite good enough no matter what. Some do both.

What successes and failures shaped your story? There are things you do well, and things that you do less well. Think about your experiences at school, the ball field, the jobs you hated, or those you enjoyed. Remember that while failure can be painful, successes are dangerous. We tend to trust in the things we do well. Perhaps you learned to accept that you are average. If so, where did that wisdom come from?

How has Jesus shaped your story? What were particular spiritual turning points, when you came more alive to Christ and followed him? This is the most important feature of your story. It is a turn from trusting in yourself and your own achievements to trusting him. It is a story about the movement from pride to humility.

How do you hope Jesus continues to grow you in wise humility? You are a person in motion. You are always growing, which is what happens when the Spirit of God works in you to enlarge your knowledge of and love for Jesus. That love reaches your relationships, work, and time. In other words, Jesus gets into all the details of your life. Imagine where you are headed with Jesus in your life.

The apostle Paul was known for short summaries of his life. Can you take the important parts of your story and condense it into a few words? Does your story have a title? Here are a few samples:

Trying to Be Someone
From Humiliation to Humility
My Need to Achieve
My Dangerous Successes
I Received Mercy

You could end your story with words similar to those of King David: "Who am I? I am unworthy of such mercy, affection, and grace, even to the point where you have crowned me as an heir with glory and honor" (2 Samuel 7:18–19, author paraphrase).

ও ও ও

CIRCLE: The main idea? Assemble those complex pieces into a simplified story.

REFLECT: Work on a five-minute version of your story.

PRAY: A good story reminds you of what God is doing and how you need him.

TALK: Most people enjoy hearing other people's stories. Who might you tell?

CONCLUSION
TRUE MANHOOD

Blessed are the poor in spirit, for theirs is the kingdom of heaven.
Blessed are those who mourn, for they shall be comforted.
Blessed are the meek, for they shall inherit the earth.
Blessed are those who hunger and thirst for righteousness,
for they shall be satisfied.
Blessed are the merciful, for they shall receive mercy.
Blessed are the pure in heart, for they shall see God.
Blessed are the peacemakers, for they shall be called sons of God.
—Matthew 5:3–9

Jesus began his teaching ministry with the blessings listed in the Sermon on the Mount. Then he lived these blessings out. These blessings effectively identified the life of Jesus and the nature of his reign and kingdom. They led with humility, even when he was warning the Pharisees. For us, they are expressed in words you considered on Day 1. Listen to them again:

"Speak, for your servant hears" (1 Samuel 3:10).
"Help" (Psalm 18:6).
"Thank you" (Psalm 52:9).
"My soul finds rest in God alone" (Psalm 62:1 NIV 1984).
"I am not worthy" (Luke 7:6).
"Jesus is Lord" (Romans 10:9).

This is the good life that we have been exploring.

Those who are poor in spirit—that is, needy before God—lead the way. All wisdom starts there. "As for me, I am poor and needy, but the Lord takes thought for me" (Psalm 40:17). Both your own sin and the times when you have been beaten down or forgotten by other people are in view. So we go to Jesus to say again, "I can bring nothing, but that is the one thing you ask—for me to bring nothing." We cannot rely on our own righteousness as we enter and participate in his kingdom. It is by grace alone. Our life is founded on the gift that God has freely given us.

Those who mourn join the poor in spirit. These people are going through hard times that they can't escape. Years ago, people interpreted hardships as God's anger. Remember Job's friends and how they blamed him for his troubles. Today, we don't need other people to say such things because our own thoughts accuse us. But these thoughts are far from the truth. God is committed to lifting up those who have been brought low. His comfort is there for the asking. Then, once you have made it past wrestling with your own hardships, you can enter the advanced course and mourn over your own sins (James 4:9), or the sins of other people: "My eyes shed streams of tears, because people do not keep your law" (Psalm 119:136). Through it all, we mourn with those who mourn.

The meek have been assured that the Lord is holy in his justice and forgiveness, and that the earth will, indeed, enjoy living under his perfect will, as heaven does now. The meek have settled in under God. Their desires for reputation and pleasure are being tamed. As a result, their anger is also restrained. They don't always have to assert their own interests because they rest in their Father.

Those with a *hunger and thirst for righteousness* have one desire that rises above the rest. Imagine what that is like. It alludes to the Lord's invitation: "Come, everyone who thirsts" (Isaiah 55:1). You know that life is only found in God and his words, and since you love him, you want to please him. Living out his words becomes a passion for you—a need. Life is rest in Christ, coupled with a restlessness to live for him.

That restlessness takes a familiar turn from life before God to life with others. Jesus identifies as blessed those who are *merciful* to the poor and needy, those who are *the pure in heart* and conduct relationships without hypocrisy, and those with a mission to be a *peacemaker* to many whose hearts or lives are in chaos.

Then true ambition rises. Jesus says to you, "You are the salt of the earth." (Matthew 5:13). He adds, "You are the light of the world" (5:14). Humility is the way to fruitfulness. When dependent people take small steps, relationships change, local communities are known by their love, and the world is turned upside down. All along the way, we can pray:

> My Father, do this in me. Give me a day that starts with, "I am poor and needy, but you take thought of me—your face is turned toward me with blessing." Give me a life that walks with humility and gentleness. Give me an evening that ends in rest because you care for me and remain awake. Father, I am yours.

ଓ ଓ ଓ

CIRCLE: Is there one thing of special importance here?

REFLECT: As an activist and spiritual warrior, what thoughts does the passage stir up for you?

PRAY: Speak the prayer above to the Lord.

TALK: Ask someone to pray for you, that humility would become a lifestyle.

ENDNOTES

1. "Expect to Be Humbled - OMF: Mission among East Asia's People." OMF International, September 15, 2023. https://omf.org/expect-to-be-humbled/.

2. Jonathan Edwards, *The Works of Jonathan Edwards* (Banner of Truth, 1974), 1:398–404.

3. C. H. Spurgeon, *C. H. Spurgeon's Autobiography: Complied from His Diary, Letters, and Records, by His Wife and His Private Secretary* (London, Passmore and Alabaster, 1897–1900), vol. 146.

4. Ayn Rand and Nietzsche are among those who despise humility, believing it is not apt for an evolutionary, dog-eat-god worldview. But their "humility" is not the same as humility before God.

5. Ward, 2003, in *Humility, Pride, and Christian Virtue Theory,* Kent Dunnington (Oxford University Press, 2018), 157

6. C. S. Lewis, *Mere Christianity* (Touchstone, 1996), 109–112.

7. Eugene Peterson, *Where Your Treasure Is: Psalms that Summon You from Self to Community* (Eerdmans, 1993), 5.

8. 1 Kings 21 is the story of a wretched king who turns to God, though not well. The Lord is so pleased with Ahab's return to himself that he tells others about it.

9. Dietrich Bonhoeffer, *The Cost of Discipleship* (SCM Press, 2015), 44.

10. Peterson, *Where Your Treasure Is*, 5.

11. James's exhortation to ask for the elders to pray for you when you are sick is more likely about a request for prayer for strength while weakened by temptation.

12. For more on shame, consider Edward Welch, *Shame Interrupted: How God Lifts the Pain of Worthlessness and Rejection* (New Growth Press, 2012); and Edward Welch, *A Small Book About Why We Hide: How Jesus Rescues Us from Insecurity, Regret, Failure, and Shame*. (New Growth Press, 2021). See also Esther Liu, *Shame: Being Known and Loved* (P&R Publishing: 2022).

13. C. S. Lewis, *Mere Christianity* (Geoffrey Bles, 1952; repr., Harper, 2001), 122.

14. Lee Ross and Andrew Ward, "Naive Realism in Everyday Life: Implications for Social Conflict and Misunderstanding," in *Values and Knowledge*, ed. E. S. Reed, E. Turiel, and T. Brown (Lawrence Erlbaum Associates Inc., 1996), 103–135, https://web.mit.edu/curhan/www/docs/Articles/15341_Readings/Negotiation_and_Conflict_Management/Ross_Ward_Naive_Realism.pdf.

ccef

CCEF is committed to restoring Christ to counseling and counseling to the church. They seek to accomplish this mission through resources, courses, events, and counseling.

To learn more or explore CCEF's resources, visit **ccef.org**.

MORE FROM EDWARD T. WELCH

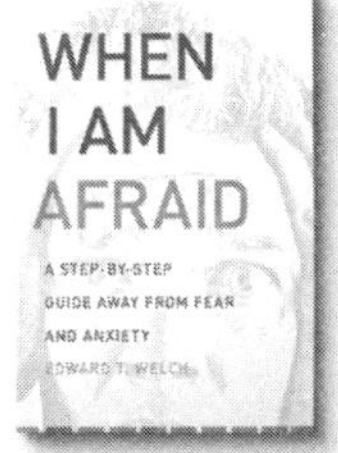